Uncommon Sense

The Wisdom of James for Dispossessed Believers

D1715808

James T. South

DEWARD
PUBLISHING COMPANY

Uncommon Sense: The Wisdom of James for Dispossessed Believers
© 2014 by DeWard Publishing Company, Ltd.
P.O. Box 6259, Chillicothe, Ohio 45601
800.300.9778
www.deward.com

All rights reserved. No portion of this book may be reproduced in any form without written permission from the publisher.

Cover design by Jonathan Hardin.

Unless otherwise noted, scripture quotations are taken from The Holy Bible, English Standard Version®, copyright ©2001 by Crossway Bibles, a publishing ministry of Good News Publishers. Used by permission. All rights reserved.

Any emphasis in Bible quotations is added.

Reasonable care has been taken to trace original sources for any excerpts and quotations appearing in this book and to document such information. For material not in the public domain, fair-use standards and practices were followed. Should any attribution be found to be incorrect or incomplete, the publisher welcomes written documentation supporting correction for subsequent printings.

Printed in the United States of America.

ISBN: 978-1-936341-66-5

With loving affection to Linda,

devoted wife, mother, and grandmother,
on the occasion of her well-deserved retirement.

She is, like James, "a servant of the Lord Jesus Christ"
and of many others as well.

Contents

Preface

I first learned to love the Letter of James in the spring of 1970 from sitting in Dr. Neil R. Lightfoot's class on "The General Epistles" at Abilene Christian University. As a new Christian contemplating a life of preaching the gospel of Christ, I entered the class starving for biblical knowledge, and I was not disappointed. Neil loved James, and as he taught it he couldn't help stopping to preach along the way (so much so that we didn't cover all the General Epistles but did get a thorough treatment of James). His enthusiasm for this great letter was infectious, and it has never left me. Over the years I have returned to James time and again for preaching and teaching material and have always been rewarded in re-studying it, and I like to think the churches where I have presented its message have benefited from it as much as I have. When a student once asked what he could do to enliven his declining old congregation, I suggested he preach an expository series of sermons from James so the church could see the practical value of in-depth Bible study. He did, and before long people were bringing their Bibles to worship, eager to hear more, and the church regained a lively spirit it had not enjoyed for many years. James has that kind of captivating power and relevance. I firmly believe all Scripture is relevant and practical, if only we learn how to understand and apply it. But James is imminently practical, so much so that its relevance almost leaps off the page as we read, and we know we are reading words that can and should make a difference in how we live.

The chapters that follow had their origin as sermons in worship settings and lessons in Bible classes, so I hope preachers and teachers will find this book especially suggestive for proclaiming James' message, although it should prove useful to anyone wanting a better understanding of his letter. Because of the intensely practical focus of James, I have written without footnotes, since they are quite impractical to most readers. Those who want to probe more deeply into what James has written will find suggestions for pursuing their goals in the works listed at the end of this Preface. I have taken the liberty of adding at the end of each chapter a verse from a relevant hymn, since it seems to me that the study of Scripture ought always to lead us into worship and since singing "songs, hymns, and spiritual songs" is itself a medium of instruction (Colossians 3.16), which only helps reinforce what we read. So if you find yourself led into a time of both study and devotion, then you will have achieved two goals rather than only one.

It's customary to begin the study of a biblical book with an introduction, discussing such topics as authorship, date of writing, intended audience, primary theological themes, etc. I have chosen not to offer such an introduction but rather discuss the matters of importance in understanding James in the first two chapters, including them as part of the exposition. James writes from the perspective of the Wisdom Literature of the Old Testament as refracted through the teachings of his elder brother, Jesus. So it is not surprising that wisdom is the dominant theme of the letter, and I have tried to bring this out in discussing each section. I cannot imagine a greater or more important theme for readers today who live in a world that seems almost totally devoid of wisdom. As the title of this book suggests, I am also persuaded that James is writing not just to Christians generally but to Christians who are dispossessed, in the sense that they live on the fringes of society and perhaps are suffering persecution or at least discrimination because of their faith. Throughout the history of our country, Christians have enjoyed a majority status and the deference that goes with it, but that circumstance has changed dramatically in recent years. Being a Christian has shifted from being an asset to being a liability (socially speaking), with many associating our faith with bigotry, hypocrisy, and a judgmental spirit; and the situation doesn't seem likely to change in the foreseeable future. This means that Christians must learn to live according to our marginalized status and to do so with all the wisdom God supplies, so that we not only hold firmly to our convictions but do so in a manner that causes others to see Jesus in us in spite of their prejudices. That's what it means to be dispossessed, and it is why James' message is so vital for our times.

Among the many works I have found helpful in studying James, I would like to mention especially Peter Davids' commentary in the New International Greek Testament Commentary series (Eerdmans, 1982), which is thorough and always helpful. James Hardy Ropes' volume in the International Critical Commentary series is now quite old (T. & T. Clark, 1916) but still useful for details of Greek grammar and syntax, and occasionally surprises with its theological insights. Hershel Shanks and Ben Witherington III have contributed an interesting study of James the man in *The Brother of Jesus: The Dramatic Story & Meaning of the First Archaeological Link to Jesus & His Family* (Harper-SanFrancisco, 2003). It includes excellent historical information about James as well as important insights into the letter, but it suffers from overconfidence in the authenticity of the "James ossuary," which created quite a stir about a decade ago but is now dismissed by most as a fake artifact. Still, it remains a very useful book for anyone interested in James. When I took Lightfoot's "General Epistles" course, we used R. V. G. Tasker's volume on James in the Tyndale New Testament Commentaries (Eerdmans, 1957). It has now been replaced by Douglas J. Moo's update in the same series (1985), which offers a solid exposition of the letter, but Tasker's volume is still worth a read by those who can get access to it. Moo followed up his shorter commentary in the Tyndale series with a lengthier study in the Pillar New Testament Commentary series (Eerdmans, 2000). Also worth reading is James Adamson's volume in the New International Commentary on the New Testament series (Eerdmans, 1976), as well as J. W. Roberts' *A Commentary on the General Epistle of James* (J. W. Roberts, 1963), which is notable for its careful exposition and helpful word studies as well as its practical applications of the letter's teachings. Commentaries that are helpful with practical application also include J. A. Motyer's *The Message of James* in the The Bible Speaks Today series (IVP, 1985), and David P. Nystrom's contribution to The NIV Application Commentary (Zondervan, 1997). There are, of course, many other good books on James, but these are some I have found to be helpful and which are worth your time.

All biblical quotations in this book are from *The Holy Bible, English Standard Version*, published by Crossway in 2001. For many years I have been an advocate of the Revised Standard Version, which has now largely passed out of common use but has been admirably replaced by the ESV, which retains the dignity and accuracy of the RSV while updating it in some important ways.

If you are a first-time reader of James, prepare yourself for some startling discoveries. James says some things you may never have heard before, because the wisdom he offers runs counter to that of the world in which we live (and of the one in which he lived). But that's precisely why we need to hear him. The "common" (in the sense of "universal") sense that prevails today is failing us miserably. We may have made dramatic leaps in technology and information and standard of living, but it is wisdom that we need. And James offers it to us in a most uncommon way. Read and be blessed.

Acknowledgments

As any writer knows, no one writes a book alone, and certainly no one publishes one alone. There are always many others who make a book possible, and it is a pleasure to acknowledge at the outset those who have helped make this book possible.

First, I would like to thank all of those who have heard these chapters (or an earlier form of them) presented orally and who have been so encouraging in their comments that I thought it would be worthwhile to write them. I'm especially grateful in this regard to my loving church family at the Glen Allen Church of Christ, who have not only listened patiently but who, by their comments, have stimulated my thinking about the meaning and application of James.

Scott Brunner is part of that family who has been especially encouraging in this regard. A gifted writer himself, he was gracious enough to read thoughtfully the first drafts of many of these chapters and make numerous helpful suggestions.

This is now the second book I have published through DeWard Publishing Company. (The first was *Just Jesus: The Evidence of History*, released in July, 2012.) In every respect Nathan Ward and Dan DeGarmo have maintained the high standards of integrity and graciousness that one looks for in a Christian publisher, and I am grateful to them for their willingness to take on this second project.

This is also my second time to work with Nathan Williams, my sharp-eyed editor at DeWard, who is a pleasure to work with, and who makes my writing better than it would otherwise be.

I am grateful to my wife, Linda, for many years of encouragement in my work of preaching, teaching, and writing, as well as for finding DeWard Publishing for me. It was on a business trip to North Carolina that she visited a congregation on a Wednesday evening and was given a DeWard book which the church was using in one of its classes, and this led to the publication of my first book with them and now this second one.

Finally, I am thankful to God for inspiring a writer like James, who in turn inspires those of us who follow Jesus to live as His servants in all that we do throughout our entire lives. If this book moves even one person in that direction, it will have been well worth the effort.

"James, a servant of God and of the Lord Jesus Christ." (1.1)

ONE | # *"James Who?"*

If some people had their way, the Letter of James wouldn't even be in the Bible. In the Fourth Century AD, the church historian Eusebius of Caesarea listed it as one of the "disputed" books which some church leaders thought should be included in the canon (the eventual list of 27 authoritative books which make up our New Testament) and others didn't. Although James eventually gained full acceptance in that discussion, the matter was far from settled in the minds of many. In the 15th Century Martin Luther famously described James as a "right strawy epistle" in comparison with the more theologically weighty letters of Paul. While he didn't leave it out of his German translation of the Bible, it's clear he had little use for it.

Even today many critics regard James not as an essentially Christian document but as a Jewish book which has been "Christianized" by the addition of two references to Jesus (1.1 and 2.1, the only places where James mentions Jesus by name). These skeptics see James as an example of Jewish Wisdom Literature, similar to Proverbs and Ecclesiastes in the Old Testament, which some early Christian scribe simply co-opted for Christian use by adding the two references to Jesus. (We shouldn't overlook the fact, however, that James makes frequent references to "the Lord" and undoubtedly has Jesus in mind in at least some of these [2.1, 4.10, 4.15, 5.7–8, 5.14–15], although clearly not in all of them [3.9, 5.10–11].)

Much of this controversy (though not by any means all of it) has centered about the question of who wrote the book. Since the author describes himself simply as "James, a servant of God and of the Lord Jesus Christ," the question naturally arises, "James who?"

Likely—and Unlikely—Candidates

First, it is entirely possible that our author is some unknown James, a figure from the early church about whom we know nothing other than the letter he left behind. But this seems unlikely since the author writes as someone who literally needs no introduction. For example, I've recently been reading a book entitled *Craddock on the Craft of Preaching.*[1] To most people this title would mean nothing because the name "Craddock" is unknown to them. But to those of us who preach and study preaching, "Craddock" can indicate only one person: Fred Craddock, widely known as one of America's foremost preachers and teachers of preachers, someone whose opinion we value highly. Our James is able to introduce himself in much the same way and for the same reason: his readers know well who he is. Add to this that the author of James speaks with a very authoritative voice, as though he were someone who rightfully expects his voice to be heard as well as someone whose opinion would be valuable to his initial readers. (Notice the large number of imperatives—commands—in this letter.) For these two reasons it seems far more likely that we should look for the author among the "Jameses" about whom we know at least something and, more importantly, whose voice the early churches would have known well and whom they would have heard gladly.

It turns out there are four Jameses in the New Testament, so our author is likely one of these. Some scholars suggest there are six men named James in the New Testament, but they count as separate people some who are very likely the same person who is mentioned in other texts. For example, Jude 1 mentions "James the brother of Jude." However, it seems probable that this is the same person as "James the Lord's brother," since Jesus had a brother named Jude as well as one named James. It is more likely the New Testament mentions only four men named James rather than six. Here are the four:

1. *James, the son of Zebedee and brother of John.* Certainly this man is one of the better-known Jameses in the early church, since he, his brother, and Peter formed a kind of inner circle among the followers of Jesus. Peter, James, and John appear together frequently in the Gospels, as at the event known as the Transfiguration (Matt 17.1–8, Mark 9.2–8, Luke 9.28–36) and when Jesus prayed in Gethsemane (Matt 26.37, Mark 14.33). He is also the one whose mother requested that her two sons have prominent places of authority once Jesus' kingdom was fully established (Matt 20.20–28). Surely such a well-known James who was so close to the Lord is a prime candidate to be the author of the Letter of James.

But there's a problem. Acts 12.1–3 reports that Herod Agrippa I, the Jewish king who ruled Judea after the death of his father Herod the Great, killed James the brother of John with the sword (i.e., had him beheaded). This event can be dated accurately as having occurred in AD 44, which is probably too early for him to be the author of the Letter of James. While it is impossible to date firmly the writing of the letter, it seems probable that it was written sometime in the early to mid-fifties AD, once the teachings of Paul had become well known among Jewish Christians.

James 2.14–26 seems to be a response to distortions of Paul's teaching on justification by faith rather than by works, and it would have taken some time for even Paul's earlier writings to have become generally known.

2. *James the son of Alphaeus.* This is that "other James" whose name appears in the lists of the apostles. He is often called (unfortunately) "James the Less" because he is less well known than the brother of John. Still, he is "one of the Twelve," so we might think he would be a good candidate to be the author of the Letter of James. However, we know nothing about him other than his name, nothing in the letter or elsewhere points to him as the author, and the book doesn't claim that its author is an apostle, so perhaps we need to keep looking.

3. *James the father of Judas (not Iscariot).* Remember there was also among the Twelve another Judas besides the one who betrayed Jesus, one whom the Gospel of Luke calls "the son of James" (6.16) and whom John 14.22 is careful to describe as "not Iscariot." This man's father was named James, but we know nothing else about him (not even if he was a believer in Jesus), so he is likely not the author for whom we are looking.

4. *James the brother of Jesus.* The James about whom we know most from the New Testament is also the most likely candidate to have written the Letter of James. Matthew 13.55 tells us that Jesus had a brother named James, which Paul also verifies in Galatians 1.19.

Before going any further, perhaps we should first clear up the question of whether or not Jesus actually had brothers. In an effort to guard the "perpetual virginity" of Mary (the belief that she never had sexual relations with Joseph but remained a virgin all her life), Roman Catholics and others have claimed that those listed as Jesus' "brothers" were actually his "cousins." However, there is a perfectly good Greek word for "cousin" (*anepsios*), but it does not occur in Matthew 13.55 or, for that matter, anywhere in the New Testament. The word used in reference to James by both Matthew and Paul is *adelphos*, the normal Greek word for "brother." Recognizing this difficulty, some have claimed that James and Jesus' other brothers were older half-brothers from Joseph's previous marriage, but there is no evidence to support such a claim. In addition Luke 2.7 refers to Jesus as Mary's "first-born son," suggesting that He was not her only child, and the New Testament actually says Jesus had four brothers and names them (Matt 13.55, Mark 6.3). So we should regard any claims that Jesus did not have brothers with a high degree of suspicion and instead take the statements of Scripture at face value.

Did Jesus' brother James have the kind of authority and notoriety to write the Letter of James? To put it simply, yes. As it turns out, he was a highly-respected leader in the early church, much more so than the other brothers of Jesus. He was popularly known, even among non-Christian Jews, as "James the Just" (or "the Righteous") because of his deep piety. Josephus, the late First-Century Jewish historian, reports his martyrdom in AD 62, an event which Josephus and, apparently, other Jews as well, viewed with disgust (*Antiquities of the Jews* 20.199–203). Notice also that in Galatians 1.19 Paul calls him not only "the Lord's brother," but also an "apostle," using the term in its wider sense of "one sent with authority," not necessarily as one of the Twelve, which he was not. Likewise, Jude (or Judas, another of Jesus' brothers) in the opening of his letter calls himself the "brother of James" without further identification, suggesting that his brother was so well known that he need say nothing further.

James' prominence comes most to the fore, however, in Acts 15 at the event known as the Jerusalem Council (or Conference).

This meeting of church leaders and others took place in AD 49 to resolve the troubling issue of whether or not Gentiles had to be circumcised in order to become Christians. The meeting included "the apostles and elders" of the church in Jerusalem (15.6), as well as Paul and Barnabas. Both Paul and Barnabas spoke, reporting the great things God had done among the Gentiles on their First Missionary Journey, and Peter reminded the assembly that God had chosen him to be the first to speak the gospel to Gentiles (a reference to the conversion of Cornelius in Acts 10). In spite of the presence of apostles and other luminaries, it was James who was apparently the chairman of the meeting. He first backed up the words of Peter with a quotation from Amos 9.11–12, then stated his judgment that Gentiles should not be required to be circumcised but rather should be admonished to avoid the excesses of paganism, a conclusion with which the assembly generally agreed and which was put into letter form for distribution among the Gentile churches. Based on this event, it is difficult to question the prominence of James as a leader among early Jewish Christians. This helps explain why Paul could refer to James as one of the three "pillars" of the Jerusalem church (Gal 2.9). James the brother of John died in AD 44, so the James of Galatians 2.9 must be "the Lord's brother," since Galatians was most likely written in 49 or later. So the answer to our question is yes, James the brother of Jesus had enough name recognition, authority, and influence to write the Letter of James and to introduce himself simply as "James, a servant of God and of the Lord Jesus Christ."

One argument against James the brother of Jesus as the author of our letter is his very literate use of Greek, which might seem unlikely for a relatively uneducated Galilean. This has led some to suggest that the basic contents of James comes from Jesus' brother but its final form is due to the work of a later editor. While not impossible, this seems an unnecessary conjecture. However, James may have used a secretary ("amanuensis" is the technical term) to write the letter as he dictated it, a practice well known from the letters of Paul (Rom 16.22, 1 Cor 16.21, Gal 6.11, Col 4.18).

Even though there is little reason to question the claim that James, the brother of Jesus and a leader of the church in Jerusalem, is the author of the Letter of James, we might wonder, if he is Jesus' brother, why didn't he identify himself that way and remove all doubt? Two factors probably explain this. One is that James, along with Jesus' other brothers, had not believed in Him during His earthly ministry (Mark 3.20–21, John 7.1–5), so that James did not feel he had any right to call himself anything other than Jesus' "servant" when he wrote the letter. The other is that Jesus made it clear in Mark 3.31–35 that physical relationship to Him counted for very little. His "brother and sister and mother" were not those who could claim blood relationship to Him, but those who, like Him, devoted themselves to doing God's will. It must have stung James' conscience to recall those words of Jesus, so much so that perhaps he could never attempt to claim any authority based on being Jesus' brother. His physical relationship to Jesus may have been significant to others, such as Paul, but to James it may have been a claim that his humility and his history would not allow him to make.

From Skeptic to Believer

We noted above that both Mark and John indicate Jesus' brothers did not believe in Him during His earthly ministry. Yet Acts 1.14 says less than fifty days after the Resurrection, "Mary the mother of Jesus, and his brothers" were worshiping alongside the apostles. How is it, then, that James came to be a follower of His brother when he had formerly been so skeptical?

It is probable that 1 Corinthians 15.7–8 holds the key. In listing the post-Resurrection appearances of Jesus (at least those of which he was aware), Paul says He "appeared to James, then to all the apostles. Last of all, as to one untimely born, he appeared also to me." It seems that James, like Paul, was granted the privilege of seeing Jesus alive following His death and Resurrection, and this removed all doubt just as it had done for Paul. The question then becomes, did Jesus make a similar appearance to His other brothers, or did James persuade them based on his vision of the risen Christ? The Bible is silent about this, so we are left to wonder. What is clear, however, is that Paul singled James out for mention, most likely because of his prominence in the early church.

Why Does It Matter?

We've just spent quite a bit of space discussing what might seem to some like a meaningless historical detail. After all, what difference does it make if James the brother of Jesus did or didn't write the Letter of James? And why is it important to know how significant James was in the early church? At first glance this might not seem very important at all, and we can certainly gain much from the letter regardless of who did or didn't write it. But let's not leave this question too quickly.

For example, isn't James' story a wonderful reminder that people's hearts can and do change? When we look at the lives of some folks, we have to wonder if anything good can ever happen with them. So many are consumed by anger, bitterness, and skepticism that it blocks them from having the abundant life Jesus talked about in John 10.10. From our perspective such people may seem hopeless—but not from God's. Jesus Himself said, "With God all things are possible." Do you remember the reaction of Saul when God first began to reveal to him that He had chosen him to be king over Israel? He asked Samuel, "Am I not a Benjaminite, from the least of the tribes of Israel? And is not my clan the humblest of all the clans of the tribe of Benjamin? Why then have you spoken to me in this way?" (1 Sam 9.21). Later his reluctance melted away, because "God gave him a new heart" (1 Sam 10.9). By God's power people do change. And James is one of those people. If Saul of Tarsus could become the apostle Paul and if Jesus' skeptical brother could become a prominent church leader, then *anyone* can, with God's help, change for the better. If this were not the case, there could be no such thing as conversion, which means "turning from one thing to another."

We need to remember this when we're discouraged about leading others to Christ. Maybe they aren't where we (and God) want them to be yet, but they can change. Remember that the message of Christ, the "gospel," is the "power of God for salvation to everyone who believes" (Rom 1.16). We also need to remember this when we're discouraged about ourselves. God isn't finished with any of us yet, and as long as we're seeking to do His will, we never know what He might make of us or do with us.

"But," someone might object, "not everyone gets to *see Jesus* as James did." True, but remember what Jesus said in John 20.29. When the once-skeptical Thomas saw the wounds in Jesus' hands and side, he declared, "My Lord and my God!" Jesus' response to Thomas gives all of us hope: "Have you believed because you have seen me? Blessed are those who have not seen and yet have believed." James, like Thomas, may have been privileged to see Jesus both before and after the Resurrection, but it is the gospel message that changes hearts. We need to believe and proclaim that gospel.

James' story also shows that past mistakes don't prevent future service. Jesus could have punished James in some way for his former unbelief, forgiven him, but then put him in some obscure corner of uselessness. That's how many believers today see themselves: unfit for service because of past mistakes, suitable only to be barely forgiven and then relegated to a back pew for life and taking no active part in the life of the church. But Jesus didn't do that with James ("a *servant* of God and of the Lord Jesus Christ"), and He doesn't want that for you either. He not only wants to save you, He wants to transform you into a valuable servant who can be a resource and a blessing for other believers. It's Satan who wants you to feel useless and unworthy so he can keep you from being fruitful in Christ's service. Don't let that happen. Remember James.

Finally, James' relationship with his divine brother shows without doubt that the only relationship with Jesus that counts for anything is a *faith* relationship. James learned that the hard way in Mark 3.31–35, when he tried to approach Jesus on the strength of being his brother in the flesh. Jesus said unequivocally that only those who join Him in serving God are truly related to Him. That should provide ample warning to all who would claim relationship to Jesus on any superficial basis, such as "I grew up in the church" or "All of my family are Christians" or "I was baptized at the age of twelve" or "I'm a Christian; I just don't go to church." It isn't these superficial claims but *doing the Father's will* that really counts.

I don't know about you, but I'm thankful that James is in the Bible. And I'm thankful to know that Jesus' brother wrote it. It gives me hope.

And can it be that I should gain an interest in my Savior's blood?
Died He for me, who caused His pain? For me who scorned His perfect love.
Amazing love!
How can it be that You, my God, would die for me?

Charles Wesley, "And Can It Be?"

"To the twelve tribes in the Dispersion." (1.1)

TWO | *A Letter to the Dispossessed*

I'm not much into technology—some of my friends would say I'm not into it at all—but I do appreciate email. It's a wonderful time-saver and a great way to communicate with lots of people all over the world. It does have its drawbacks, however. One is, it's easy to send a message to someone you hadn't intended (been there, done that), and another is you get lots of stuff from people you don't know about things of no interest or applicability to you.

When James wrote his letter he didn't have that problem. From the letter itself we can tell he knew well the people to whom he wrote. He calls them "my brothers" some 14 times, and in 3 of these it's "my *beloved* brothers." He knew who they were and what they needed to hear, so he's very specific about what he says. Likewise they knew and respected him and so were willing to hear what he had to say.

Probably Jewish

So who were the people who first laid eyes on the Letter of James, the ones James had in mind as he wrote? Unlike the letters of Paul, James doesn't begin with the "sender-to-recipient" formula (see 1 Thess 1.1 for an example) that might tell us specifically who they were and where they lived. Still, James does offer some clues.

First, they were apparently Jewish Christians, possibly living outside Palestine. In 1.1 James calls them "the twelve tribes in the Dispersion. (See the similar phrase "exiles of the dispersion" in 1 Peter 1.1.) The "Dispersion" (or "Diaspora" as it's sometimes called, transliterating the Greek word *diaspora*) was the scattering of the Jewish people which began with the Assyrian invasion of Israel in 721 BC. It was the custom of the Assyrians, as of many ancient empires, to deliberately displace the most capable citizens of captured nations and cities and to replace them with displaced people from other lands they had conquered. The effect was to break any remaining spirit of nationalism that might remain and possibly lead to a revolt, as well as to remove all of those most likely to successfully carry out such a rebellion. In addition, it gave the captors the benefits of the skills and knowledge of the best and brightest from many nations. The Babylonians, who eventually succeeded in conquering the Assyrians, continued this practice and displaced even more Jews following the destruction of Jerusalem and its Temple in 586 BC. In fact the Dispersion continues even today, since the vast majority of Jews still live outside Palestine.

So in 1.1 is James speaking literally or figuratively? There are several possibilities, and it's impossible to know for sure exactly what James meant, but I think we can get pretty close.

1. He could be speaking entirely literally. In that case the "twelve tribes" represent Jewish Christians scattered outside Palestine.

2. He could be speaking entirely figuratively. From this perspective the "twelve tribes" are Christians generally, not just Jewish ones. Since the New Testament presents the church as the "New Israel," this would be an appropriate way to speak of believers of all nationalities (see Galatians 6.16, along with the fact that

Jesus built the church on the "foundation" of twelve apostles, corresponding to the twelve tribes of Israel, as reflected in Revelation 21.12–14). From a figurative point of view, these multi-national believers would be dispersed everywhere, both in and outside Palestine. The "nations" among whom they are scattered would then represent non-believers.

3. James' reference could be partly literal and partly figurative. The "twelve tribes" could be a reference specifically to Jewish believers, but "the Dispersion" could refer to wherever these believers might be scattered, not just outside Palestine. In fact, they could even be *in* Palestine but still "scattered" among the unbelievers there.

There is nothing implausible about any of these reconstructions, and not a great deal is at stake in the overall interpretation of the letter regardless of what we conclude about 1.1. However, some features of the letter suggest that, although what James writes equally applies to all believers, his intended audience is Jewish Christians.

One of these features is the style of the letter, which reminds us very much of the Wisdom Literature of the Old Testament (Job, Psalms, Proverbs, Ecclesiastes, Song of Solomon). It's difficult for an experienced Bible student to read a section such as James 1.19–27 without calling to mind the short, pithy sayings found in Proverbs. And remember that James is a book primarily about wisdom (1.5, 3.13–18). Jewish readers would quickly pick up on this and feel right at home with James' writing and teaching style.

Another feature of the letter makes it all but certain that James is writing to Jewish Christians. In 2.2, as he chastises his readers for their shabby treatment of impoverished visitors to their worship services and their more respectful treatment of the rich, James calls their assembly a "synagogue." The Greek word *syna-*

gogue means an assembly or gathering. We associate "synagogue" with Jewish places of worship, but its meaning isn't limited to that. Some assume James was writing to a group of Christians who were actually meeting in a synagogue for their place of worship, but it seems unlikely that Jewish authorities would have allowed Christian worship to take place in their facilities (although for much of the First Century AD Jewish Christians continued to participate in the normal synagogue services on the Sabbath in addition to their specifically Christian worship assemblies on Sunday). It's more likely that James 2.2 reflects a time when Jewish Christians still called their Christian worship assemblies "synagogues," a practice they soon abandoned as hostilities arose between them and Jewish religious leaders. James 2.2 is the only place in the New Testament where a Christian assembly is called a "synagogue," which suggests an early date for the writing of the letter. More importantly for our purposes of trying to identify James' first readers, it suggests they were most likely Jewish Christians and not Gentiles. Where they lived we do not know, as James gives no geographical clues that might tell us, although there are some agricultural references that might suggest they lived in a rural area (3.12, 3.18, 5.4, 5.7), but even this is uncertain.

Suffering Trials

The first topic James addresses is how to face trials in the proper spirit (1.2–4), suggesting that suffering was perhaps the most distinguishing characteristic of his readers. In fact much of what James says in the letter relates to trials and how to endure them, a thought that never seems far from his mind (1.12–15). While certainly these believers would have suffered the "various kinds" of trials common to all Christians (persecution, illness, financial strain, temptation, etc.), the letter reveals a particularly grievous form of trial which they had to endure: oppression by the rich.

One notable feature of James is that the rich never come off looking good at all and are, in fact, roundly condemned as a group. The poor, on the other hand, seem to be the particular objects of God's blessings. In 2.5–7 James says explicitly that the rich were dragging these believers into court (perhaps to wrest control of their land from them?) and blaspheming the name of Christ (making it virtually certain they were not rich Christians). Likewise in 5.1–6 James sternly rebukes the rich for such sins as hoarding their wealth, defrauding poor laborers of their pay, self-indulgence, and even the "murder" of the righteous. Modern readers are often shocked at that last accusation, especially when they make the mistake of assuming that these rich people were part of the church, an assumption based on the fact that they are addressed in the letter. However, as we will see when we look more closely at chapter 5, this assumption is not likely to be correct, although there were surely at least a few rich people in the church. It was common in ancient Jewish literature to speak of the righteous as "the poor" and the rich as "the unrighteous." Notice that 5.6 accuses the rich specifically of murdering "the righteous person," not "the poor person." On the other hand, the description of the behavior of the rich toward the poor in 2.5–7 and 5.1–6 does suggest economic oppression, so in this instance "the poor" probably are poor, not just in spirit but also materially.

Dispossessed

So the picture that emerges of James' first readers is this they were Jewish Christians, probably living outside Palestine, who were (mostly) economically poor and oppressed by the wealthier people around them. For this reason James is sometimes described as "a letter to the dispossessed," since it speaks primarily to people who were suffering the forms of oppression that normally go with the abuse of the poor by the rich. We can well imagine that some of them had been booted off their land, that others had been robbed of their wages, and that some had even been starved to death by their wealthy land-holding neighbors. It is the kind of scene that occurs repeatedly wherever there is a large gap between rich and poor and in the absence of a genuine middle class.

James' goal, as we will see beginning in 1.5, is to instruct such oppressed people how to live by God's wisdom even in the midst of their experience of being dispossessed by those more powerful than themselves. Because of this James has a powerful message to the vast majority of people of the world, most of whom live with exactly this sort of oppression. In this regard James echoes the sentiments of the author of Ecclesiastes who wrote,

> Moreover I saw under the sun that in the place of justice, even there was wickedness, and in the place of righteousness, even there was wickedness. I said in my heart, God will judge the righteous and the wicked, for there is a time for every matter and for every work.... Again I saw all the oppressions that are done under the sun. And behold, the tears of the oppressed, and they had no one to comfort them! On the side of their oppressors there was power, and there was no one to comfort them. And I thought the dead who are already dead more fortunate than the living who are still alive. But better than both is he who has not yet been and has not seen the evil deeds that are done under the sun. (Eccl 3.16–17, 4.1–3).

Whoever James' first readers were and wherever they lived, they would surely have nodded their heads in agreement with these tragic and depressing words.

"But That's Not Me—Or Is It?"

To those of us who are not among the dispossessed of the world, who live in comfortable houses and drive wherever we want and are more likely to be concerned about the expansion of our waist-lines than where our next meal is coming from, the words of James and Ecclesiastes can seem foreign and irrelevant. After all, people who can afford to purchase iPads and Smart Phones—or even this book—generally aren't suffering the kinds of oppression that James describes. So of what value is James' message to us? Was it intended only for an ancient audience of cast-off people or, perhaps more broadly, for them and their modern contemporaries as well? Does it have a message for the affluent of this world whose wages come regularly and whose rights are generally protected rather than trampled? I strongly believe it does—but it's a message you may not enjoy hearing.

What I'm suggesting is this: Although we may not *be* among the world's dispossessed, we would do well to learn to live as though we *were*, because it may not be long until we *are*. There are ways other than economic oppression to be on the fringes of your culture. American society has done a drastic turn-around in the past 50 years in its attitude toward Christian faith. Many of us grew up in a world where both our faith and our Scriptures were respected, even by those who did not themselves pay much attention to them. In our lifetimes we have seen such activities as daily Bible reading in public school go from being normal to being criminal. Our society is rapidly turning, not just *away from* a Christian world view but *against* that world view and the faith which underlies it. Whereas Christians once battled indifference toward Christ, we now face increasing hostility toward Him. Tenets of basic morality are now not only ignored but are responded to in anger from those who refuse to be bound by any moral requirements. If these trends continue—and there is every reason to believe they will—then we who believe will continually find ourselves marginalized by our culture. Already there are those who actively seek to suppress what we believe, which means that, if they get their way, we will become the oppressed minority in our society. That being the case, we not only can find something of value in James, we desperately *need* the wisdom he offers. We need his wisdom for the dispossessed every bit as much as did his first readers.

So What's the Message?

Putting ourselves in the place of James' first readers, what does he say to us, to those who may not be dispossessed but may soon become so?

1. *First, don't cry about it.* James' first word of wisdom to the dispossessed is to "Count it all joy when you meet trials of various kinds" (1.2). Even though circumstances may be tough, the proper response is not to whine about them but rather to respond in faith. In saying this, James is reflecting the teachings of his elder brother who said, "Blessed are you when others revile you and persecute you and utter all kinds of evil against you falsely on my account. Rejoice and be glad, for your reward is great in heaven, for so they persecuted the prophets who were before you" (Matt 5.11–12). Luke 6.26 puts an even more interesting spin on suffering: "Woe to you when all people speak well of you, for so their fathers did to the false prophets." Having society's approval isn't necessarily a good thing; it may mean we aren't living up to our calling. Living faithfully for Christ in times of oppression won't win you any popularity contests. But when you're on the "losing" end of persecution you should know you're really in fabulous company: the prophets of old who were notoriously persecuted and even killed by their contemporaries (Matthew 23.37, Acts 7.51–52) and, of course, Jesus Himself. In fact, being rejected by the world is one of the hallmarks of a follower of Jesus according to John 15.18–20.

So it isn't a tragedy to be dispossessed by a world that rejects Christ. Rather, it's an honor, and we should "count it all joy." That doesn't mean that such rejection doesn't hurt; it simply means we're able to see it in a larger and different context than the event itself. We can see it for what it is, an indication that we're on the right track by following Jesus.

2. *Even when you're oppressed, God expects you to live responsibly.* Experiencing hardship is no excuse for failing to treat others in a Christ-like way. No matter what you're going through, others have problems of their own and don't need you to become one of them. In 1.22 James urges us to "be doers of the word and not hearers only." In 3.1–4.12 James devotes a lengthy section of the letter to the problem of believers' mistreatment of one another. Apparently the pressure was getting to them, and they weren't living out their Christian calling to love and serve one another as they should. James chastises them for this distorted reaction to their circumstances and reminds them of their responsibility to one another—regardless of what was going on in their lives.

3. *Being dispossessed in this world should make you more heavenly-minded.* James climaxes his letter by urging us to take the long view of our circumstances—not just what's happening now but where all of it will eventually lead. Patience (better, "steadfast-ness," the refusal to give up) is necessary in order to have that long view, for it keeps us from looking at life in the same materialistic and self-serving way that non-believers do. Taking the long view reminds us that we are living not only in and for this world, but for the next, where we will be completely at home with God and without all of the trials that plague us now.

So it turns out that James is very much a letter to us and about us, not just to struggling Christians 2,000 years ago but to struggling Christians now. The struggles we face are not so different from what they faced, and as time goes on ours will likely become even more like theirs. And the wisdom James offers is every bit as appropriate for our situation as for theirs. So when we hear James say, "Listen, my beloved brothers," we should be "quick to hear" (1.19).

Gentle Shepherd, come and lead us, For we need You to help us find our way.
Gentle Shepherd, come and feed us, For we need Your strength from day to day.
There's no other we can turn to Who can help us face another day;
Gentle Shepherd, come and lead us. For we need You to help us find our way.

Gloria Gaither, "Gentle Shepherd"

"Count it all joy, my brothers, when you meet trials of various kinds." (1.2–4)

THREE | *An Abnormal Reaction to Normal Circumstances*

Do you remember when you first became a Christian? Remember that rush of joy, enthusiasm, perhaps even idealism, that you had about the Christian life and about other Christians?

Remember when reality began to hit? How you soon discovered that you still had struggles and made mistakes and that other Christians weren't perfect either? Do you remember the first time you realized there were actually people who opposed your faith and convictions? That reality has never gone away, has it? There are always struggles in living for Christ. The principle of "Everything that can go wrong, will" may be too pessimistic, but there are always obstacles. Somehow there always seems to be some fly in our spiritual ointment, no matter how hard we try to make it otherwise.

Well, there's nothing new about that. James realized it was a problem in the earliest days of the church, and in 1.2–4 he writes to give insight that we need and can use as we face hardships. James' wisdom about trials can be summed up in three statements:

(1) Hardship is inevitable.
(2) Joy is always possible.
(3) Steadfastness is invaluable.

1. Hardship is inevitable. Notice that James begins the body of his letter in verse 2 by saying, "Count it all joy...*when* you meet various trials"—not *if* you meet various trials. He's simply acknowledging the reality that no one escapes hardship in living for Christ. In place of "trials" the King James Version says "temptations." It's true that we all encounter temptations too, but that isn't James' point here. The Greek word *peirasmoi* has a broader meaning than "temptations," although it can include them. Rather it means all kinds of hardships, challenges, and obstacles to faith. This includes such things as illness, financial struggles, difficult relationships, persecution, and the uncertainties of life in this world. All of us will meet these trials at some (or even many) points in life.

Notice how vastly different this is from the "Health and Wealth Gospel" (*aka* "Prosperity Gospel") so many preach today. There are plenty out there who try to persuade you that a *real* Christian simply doesn't face the hardships that other folks do. If our faith is intact, we are told, we won't encounter physical illness or financial setbacks. All we have to do (assuming we're *really* right with the Lord) is "name it and claim it," and God will give us whatever our hearts desire. Naturally, much of this teaching centers on material and financial gains. Some even go so far as to claim that Jesus was a rich man and therefore He wants all His followers to be rich as well.

While such ideas may appeal to many, they totally contrast to what the Bible actually says. For example, do you recall what Isaiah predicted about our Lord, that He would be "a man of sorrows and acquainted with grief"? That statement alone sufficiently proves the falsehood of the "Health and Wealth" mentality, especially when we realize that the Hebrew word for "grief" in Isaiah 53.3 can also be translated "sickness" (see the ESV footnote). Isaiah says Jesus experienced sorrows, grief, and even sickness here on this earth. Likewise the Old Testament prophets were reviled, rejected, even killed—not because there was something lacking in their faith but because they *were* faithful to God (Matt 23.29–31, Acts 7.51–52). Second Corinthians 11.22–29 contains an amazing catalogue of the sufferings Paul experienced, including beatings, shipwreck, and imprisonment. What would the Health and Wealth people say was lacking in *his* faith? Peter wrote his first letter to believers who were "aliens and exiles" in this world of unbelief and told them not to be surprised at the "fiery trial" that would surely come upon them to test them, but never did he berate them for a faulty faith (1 Pet 4.12–14).

The question is not "Will you experience trials in this life?" but "How will you respond when trials come upon you?" How do you keep those trials from becoming temptations that erode faith? This leads to James' second assertion.

2. *Joy is always possible.* Much to the surprise of many, James calls for what might be described as an abnormal response to a normal situation. "Count it all joy, my brothers, when you meet trials of various kinds." As we have seen, trials are the norm. But responding to those trials with joy is not. How can James possibly say such a thing? Is he being hopelessly unrealistic?

The word "count" (verse 2) means to "consider it all joy" when you experience trials. It has to do with how we choose to perceive what is happening to us and how we decide to respond to it. What this tells us is, our circumstances don't necessarily determine our state of mind or our attitude of life. We've all seen people who faced incredible hardships, yet did so with cheerful optimism and gratitude for life. At the same time, others face far less formidable circumstances but are negative, complaining, and pessimistic. The difference? The decision each one makes regarding his or her outlook on suffering.

Part of our problem with grasping what James is getting at here is a failure to understand what "joy" means. Joy isn't the same as pleasure or happiness. Sometimes Bible translations fail us by giving too-easy definitions of words and mislead us in the process. For example, the Revised English Bible translates James 1.2 this way: "Count yourselves supremely happy" in facing trials. But there is a huge difference between happiness and joy. Happiness is an emotional response to circumstances, but joy is an attitude of the heart that can see the potential for good even in a bad situation and be thankful for it. Joy doesn't depend on the circumstances themselves but on our response to them. No one is going to be happy about being sick or abused, but we can be joyful in spite of suffering such things because we see beyond them to greater blessings.

Still we have to ask, "How is joy *always* possible?" How can James speak so concretely about every experience of trial? It has to do with the connection between joy and faith: We know that in God's hands even the worst of experiences has the potential to work out for our good. Don't overlook the word "for" in 1.3. Here's the reason for joy in the face of trial: our trials amount to a testing of our faith, which produces steadfastness. And (v 4) steadfastness leads us to wholeness so that we are "lacking in nothing." Let's unpack that for a moment.

When James says that trials "test" our faith, he doesn't mean they are attempts to break us or to see how much we can take before caving in or a test to see if we really have any faith. Rather, trials temper us like intense heat tempers steel to make it stronger. That only happens through the application of heat, but the result is a better implement. So when we endure a trial, whatever faith we have becomes stronger, better faith. Underlying all of this is the conviction that our God can do anything, even use our worst circumstances for a good purpose—and in *that* we rejoice. Here are some biblical examples of this principle.

In the Sermon on the Mount Jesus told His disciples they would be "blessed" when persecuted, reviled, and lied about: "Rejoice and be glad, for your reward is great in heaven, for so they persecuted the prophets who were before you" (Matt 5.11–12). Hebrews 12.1–2 urges us to lay aside sin so we can run our "race" with endurance. Our example is Jesus, "who for the joy that was set before him endured the cross, despising the shame, and is seated at the right hand of the throne of God." There was never any greater suffering or injustice than what Jesus experienced on the Cross, but neither was there ever so much good accomplished. And Peter urged those struggling "aliens and exiles" to whom he wrote to accept the testing of their faith for the same reasons James gives and adds, "Though you do not now see him, you believe in him and rejoice with joy that is inexpressible and filled with glory, obtaining the outcome of your faith, the salvation of your souls" (1 Pet 1.3–9).

James' point is this: You're going to experience hardship, so let God use it to make you better. And that is cause for rejoicing.

3. Steadfastness is invaluable. Joy in the face of suffering is possible because we are convinced something good will come from it. This isn't the same as saying "Everything happens for a purpose," a glib answer often given supposedly to comfort those undergoing trials. If the saying were true, we'd have to ask, "Whose purpose?" It isn't that all suffering is somehow a detail in the canvas of God's plan for our lives (although some suffering certainly may be), which would suggest that God causes the suffering. Rather, God displays His greatness by taking even the worst situations and causing something good to come from them.

In the immediate sense in which James is speaking, that something good is "steadfastness." As I mentioned above, "steadfastness" is a better translation of James' word *hupomone* than is "patience." Patience implies some degree of passivity, a willingness to wait. We usually think of "patient" people as those who stoically accept whatever happens (which isn't most of us!). "Steadfastness," on the other hand, means hanging in there and refusing to be stopped no matter what happens. (Remember the Persistent Widow in Jesus' parable, Luke 18.1–8?) Especially in this context it suggests a refusal to stop trusting God and His goodness. It is the testing of our faith that produces such dogged determination and the strength to go with it to enable us to endure.

How important is it to be steadfast? James says there's no salvation without it (1.12), and Paul says we cannot please God without it (Rom 2.7) and love can't be genuine without it (1 Cor 13.7), so it must be pretty important. In fact, it isn't saying too much to put it this way: *the only spiritually fatal mistake a Christian can make is to give up.* Paul urges us in Galatians 6.9–10 not to grow weary in doing good, "for in due season we will reap *if we do not give up.*" That being the case, anything that helps produce steadfastness within us must be counted as a blessing. Paul sounds much like James when he says in Romans 5.1–5,

> Therefore, since we have been justified by faith, we have peace with God through our Lord Jesus Christ. Through him we have also obtained access by faith into this grace in which we stand, and we rejoice in hope of the glory of God. More than that, we rejoice in our sufferings, knowing that suffering produces endurance [*hupomone*], and endurance produces character, and character produces hope, and hope does not put us to shame, because God's love has been poured into our hearts through the Holy Spirit who has been given to us.

So we should welcome the full effect of steadfastness in our lives, because it is bringing us to spiritual wholeness so that we are "lacking in nothing." This doesn't mean we obtain absolute moral and spiritual perfection. Such a concept is foreign to the Bible other than when speaking of God and Christ. Rather, it means we become what God calls us to be, and eventually even absolute wholeness is ours once we've endured to the end and arrived safely at home with God (v 12).

Is the response to trials that James calls for a normal one? No, not for most people. But for the believer in Christ it makes perfectly good sense. Knowing all that Jesus accomplished through His suffering and death, and knowing that our God is sufficient to make good come from even the worst of circumstances, we have every reason to "count it all joy" when we meet trials of various kinds.

Remember: Hardship is inevitable. Joy is always possible. Steadfastness is invaluable. The wise believer will have no trouble responding with a hearty "Amen!"

God has smiled on me, He has set me free;
God has smiled on me, He's been good to me.
Dark clouds rolled away, Sunshine now on me;
God has smiled on me, He's been good to me.

Unknown and Alton Howard, "God Has Smiled On Me"

"If any of you lacks wisdom, let him ask God." (1.5–11)

FOUR | *Wisdom from a Generous God*

The American humorist and television personality Sam Levenson once said, "It's so simple to be wise. Just think of something stupid to say and then don't say it." Unfortunately, it's not quite that simple, and wisdom is a commodity which most find hard to come by. There certainly doesn't seem to be an abundance of it in the world in general.

We've been saying all along in our study of James that his overriding idea is wisdom, and now in verse five he mentions it by name for the first time. It's no accident that this first mention comes just after his encouragement to "count it all joy" when suffering trials because of the realization that trials test our faith and produce steadfastness and steadfastness leads us to spiritual wholeness. Easy enough to say, but it takes wisdom to recognize such a profound (and profoundly difficult) truth. So when James says, "If any of you lacks wisdom," he isn't speaking of wisdom in a vacuum or in the abstract. He's talking about the wisdom especially needed by dispossessed people who are trying to cope with life's struggles. In reality, he's talking to and about all of us. Who *doesn't* need wisdom to navigate the complexities of today's world?

Wisdom's Source

Getting wisdom may not be nearly so complex a process as we imagine. In fact, James makes it sound extremely simple: "Ask God…and it will be given." The sticking point here for many is going to the right source for wisdom. Mass media bombards us with experts who offer their two cents' worth on everything from finances to fitness to feeling good about ourselves. But in spite of the prevalence of expert advice, how much wisdom do most people actually have? Not much, I'm afraid. The kind of wisdom being offered up today falls more into the category of what Paul describes as "the wisdom of this age" (1 Cor 2.6; see James' contrast between the "wisdom that comes down from above" *versus* that which is "earthly, unspiritual, demonic" in 3.13–15). The right source for obtaining wisdom isn't the most recent guest on the most-watched TV talk show, but God Himself. Wisdom isn't the same as information, nor is it education or even experience. All of these can be tools for gaining wisdom, but none is sufficient by itself. We might characterize wisdom as *the ability to see reality for what it really is and not what it appears to be* (as in the example in vv 9–11). It's *knowing how to live in this world in order to obtain the highest result rather than the most immediately gratifying one.* Wisdom is seeing what others don't see because they aren't looking at life from God's perspective. Wisdom is God's gift to His people.

Look how James characterizes God in identifying Him as the true source of wisdom. First, He "gives generously to all." The Greek word *haplos*, usually translated as "generously," literally means "simply" or "openly"; we might say that God's giving is focused; He *wants* us to have His wisdom, so He just gives it to us. God as the source of wisdom wouldn't have been a new thought to James' Jewish readers, since Proverbs 2.6 says, "For the Lord gives wisdom; from his mouth come knowledge and understanding."

Proverbs 8 personifies Wisdom as a woman calling out and pleading with the simple to pay heed to her in order to avoid disaster in life. And all devout Jews would have known the story of God's gift of wisdom to King Solomon in 1 Kings 3. What James offers isn't something new but a reminder that giving and giving generously is fundamental to God's nature. In addition, God doesn't give His wisdom only to some but to all who ask Him. And when God gives, He doesn't do so in the same way we sometimes do ("What? Again!?"). Rather, He gives "without reproaching" and doesn't scold or rebuke us for asking Him again and again. On the contrary, He invites us to do so, as He's doing in this verse. The promise of James 1.5 is clear and absolute: "it will be given him." God never shuts the door on those who come seeking His wisdom.

Does that mean you and I can just say, "Lord, make me wise," and suddenly we will be? Not usually, although we shouldn't rule out the possibility that in a particularly stressful situation God will simply infuse us with the necessary wisdom for our circumstances. Sometimes we don't have much time to decide the right thing to do, and we should believe that if we call on God, He will help us. But in most cases wisdom comes over a period of time, sometimes a lengthy one, and it may involve a combination of factors including prayer, Scripture reading, evaluating our options, advice from other believers (especially wise ones), and experience. Attaining wisdom often involves going through hardship (maybe the "trials of various kinds" James mentions in 1.2). It has often been observed that asking for wisdom can be a mixed blessing, because it may not come without some struggles. Still, unless we're asking God for wisdom, we may go through all sorts of hardships and come out being none the wiser for it, and there's no wisdom in that.

On One Condition…

No sooner has James given the assurance of wisdom as God's gift than he states the one requirement for obtaining it: faith. "But let him ask in faith, with no doubting" (v 6). This requirement is absolute, because James goes on to say that doubters can't be assured of receiving anything from the Lord (vv 7–8). He compares doubters to the restless surface of the sea, always in a state of flux, unstable, flowing one direction then ebbing in another. He describes such people as "double-minded," or literally "two-souled." Their minds are never clearly made up in God's direction, but rather they are constantly vacillating between faith and unbelief.

I'm afraid a misunderstanding of James 1.6–8 sometimes keeps people from praying, and that's a tragedy. What happens is we realize our faith isn't perfect, that we sometimes pray while at the same time not being sure whether God will answer our prayer or not. Is God really willing to do this? Am I asking too much? Is my prayer in line with God's will? When we read James' words about doubting and being double-minded, we conclude that our prayers would be ineffective and that we'll receive nothing from God, so why bother? All of us are to some extent like the desperate father in Mark 9.24 who cried out, "Lord, I believe. Help my unbelief!" We frequently demonstrate the smallness of our faith by asking God for so little, or we are actually surprised when He answers and grants our requests. These are examples of the *weakness* of our faith but not of double-mindedness. Clearly, all doubt is not the same.

James is talking about someone who simply can't (or won't) make up his mind about God, who toys with the idea of God but remains uncommitted to Him. The concept is based on the Old Testament idea of a heart divided between God and some "other god." In 1 Kings 18.21 Elijah challenged the Israelites who persisted in dabbling in idolatry, "How long will you go limping between two different opinions? If the Lord is God, follow him; but if Baal, then follow him." They revealed their stubbornly divided loyalty by the fact that they "did not answer him a word"; that is, they remained uncommitted either way. This trying to walk in two different directions at once is what James means by "double-minded." Such a person has no "anchor of the soul," and his or her loyalty to God is constantly in doubt. A person like that receives nothing from God. But God never refuses wisdom to His children who love Him and seek it from Him—and we should never hesitate to ask, since Jesus said that God honors even the smallest of faith (Matt 7.19–20).

A Wise Outlook on Wealth

James immediately follows his words about wisdom with a pertinent example: how we view our place in this world based on our material possessions, or the lack of them. As in verse 2, he again says something that sounds contradictory: "Let the lowly brother boast in his exaltation, and the rich in his humiliation" (v 9). Shouldn't that be the other way around? Isn't it the rich in this world who have something to boast about, and aren't the lowly (poor) those who are often embarrassed by their lack of material things? Not when you have sought and obtained wisdom from God. James is clearly advising a great reversal of the way we perceive the world, a perspective that comes when we have wisdom from God. So what is he getting at?

First, we should note that James speaks of "the lowly *brother*" and not of lowly people in general. Although he doesn't specify "the rich *brother*," the context suggests that in cases of both rich and poor he is thinking of believers; otherwise they wouldn't stand a chance of having the kind of wisdom he's talking about. Both lowly and rich have some grounds for boasting; it's what they each boast about that makes James' advice sound so odd. These verses are a vivid reminder that the truly wise person knows just how important wealth really *isn't.* What really counts is realizing the great spiritual wealth we have because of Christ so that even the lowliest believer is rich in the sight of God and ought to be so in his own eyes as well. Likewise, the rich (brother), in spite of his great material wealth, knows just how impoverished he truly is apart from the blessings that come from knowing Christ. He should rejoice in this knowledge because of the wisdom he has gained and because he now has the true riches of life, not just the material ones. In saying this James reflects the teachings of Jesus, who said, "For what will it profit a man if he gains the whole world and forfeits his life? Or what shall a man give in return for his life?" (Matt 16.26).

Notice at this point that James continues talking about the rich person without saying any more about the poor brother. In particular he emphasizes the temporary nature, not of wealth, but of life itself. Perhaps he does so because this is a lesson especially difficult for the rich to learn. The poor, who often live on the margins of survival, know well the fragile nature of life. Life is no less fragile for the rich, but their wealth often masks this fact because they have so many alternative resources to fall back on. So James reminds us that the rich fade "like the flower of the grass," which in spite of its beauty is quickly scorched by the hot sun and vanishes in a matter of hours. "So also will the rich man fade away in the midst of his pursuits." The Bible is rich with imagery stressing the brevity of human existence, and this is not James' only use of it. In 4.14 he says life is but a "mist that appears for a little time and then vanishes." In saying this, he echoes the Old Testament Wisdom Literature which makes the brevity and fragility of life something of a theme. "Remember that my life is a breath," Job said, "my eye will never again see good" (Job 7.7).

And David wrote,

> O Lord, make me know my end
>> and what is the measure of my days;
>> let me know how fleeting I am!
> Behold, you have made my days a few handbreadths,
>> and my lifetime is as nothing before you.
> Surely all mankind stands as a mere breath! (Psa 39.4–5)

Chances are, such texts as these that describe our lives as fog, mist, vapor, clouds, and breath are not anybody's favorite Bible verses. But divine wisdom impresses their truthfulness on us. We need to know just how fleeting life really is, especially the more wealth we have, because we may be tempted to think it somehow puts us into a different category from the homeless person on the street, but it doesn't. The rich man, James says, "will…fade away in the midst of his pursuits." Don't overlook that little phrase "in the midst of"; it reminds us that life isn't over only when we think we're finished with it. It's just over when it's over, and no amount of wealth or possessions will change that.

If that reality isn't part of your thinking, perhaps it's time you asked God for wisdom. According to James, God will undoubtedly make you know your end and the measure of your days, a major factor in being wise.

I'd rather have Jesus than silver or gold,
I'd rather be His than have riches untold;
I'd rather have Jesus than houses or lands,
I'd rather be led by His nail-pierc'd hand
Than to be the king of a vast domain or be held in sin's dread sway;
I'd rather have Jesus than anything this world affords today.

Rhea F. Miller, "I'd Rather Have Jesus"

"Let no one say when he is tempted, 'I am being tempted by God.'" (1.12–18)

FIVE | *Where Temptation* Doesn't *Come From*

Do you remember the story of what we usually call "The Fall" in Genesis 3? Satan (in the guise of a serpent) entered God's beautiful new creation and deceived Eve, who in turn tempted Adam so that they both sinned. Whereas there had once been peace and harmony in the garden, there was now shame and fear, so much so that when Adam and Eve "heard the sound of the Lord God walking in the garden in the cool of the day," they hid themselves from Him (Gen 3.8). No longer was there unbroken fellowship and joy in His presence; something had changed. When God quizzed the man, attempting to get him to confess what he had done, Adam responded by blaming his wife—and, by extension, God Himself: "The woman *whom you gave to be with me*, she gave me the fruit of the tree, and I ate" (Gen 3.12). It was an audacious accusation, to say the least, to accuse the Creator of planting the seeds of failure by giving Eve to Adam. Just a few verses before, he had exclaimed joyfully over his new companion: "This at last is bone of my bones and flesh of my flesh; she shall be called Woman, because she was taken out of man" (Gen 2.23). Now he's blaming God for this very gift. There was no wisdom in that, and James wants to be sure that his readers don't make the same mistake or that they stop making it if they already were doing so.

The Wisdom to Remain Steadfast

At the outset of his letter James introduces the twin themes of trials and steadfastness (1.2–4), apparently because suffering trials was the common experience of his readers. Wisdom will cause the sufferer to understand that there is an up side to undergoing trials, because tests of faith produce steadfastness, which is a step toward spiritual wholeness. In verse 12 James picks up these threads again and continues his discussion of the advantages of steadfastness. This time he pronounces blessing on the man who remains steadfast while enduring trial, because the outcome is receiving the "crown of life." (See 1 Cor 9.25, 2 Tim 4.8, 1 Pet 5.4 for additional references to salvation as a "crown.") This isn't the royal crown of a ruler but the victor's crown bestowed on the winner of an athletic contest (Greek, *stephanos*), usually a laurel wreath, leading to the New Testament's emphasis on the Christian's crown as "imperishable" or "unfading" in contrast to earthly rewards.

Notice James' emphasis on the source of this crown: "which God has promised to those who love him." In addition to giving His wisdom and strength to those who struggle, God also provides a glorious crown at the end of it all. As James goes ahead to declare, it's just His nature to do that sort of thing. It *isn't* His nature to lead us into sin.

Don't Even Think About It!

Part of the steadfastness James says we should have is the ability to endure trials without turning against God in the process. Particularly when trials go on for a long period of time, exasperation sometimes causes us to question God's goodness and causes some even to blame Him for allowing trials into our lives. At this point, our trials become temptations, and we are making God the responsible party for the whole thing. Likewise blaming God is a handy way to evade our own responsibility for our sins: if God tempts, who can resist?

There's no question that God allows negative circumstances to come into our lives, otherwise they wouldn't be there. But that isn't the same as saying God tempts us, that His aim is to trip us up or bring about our spiritual downfall. Rather, as James said earlier, He uses these trials to strengthen us. If they become something other than that, it isn't God's fault, and we shouldn't try to pin the blame on Him. Why? Because it isn't in God's nature to tempt us. "God cannot be tempted with evil, and he himself tempts no one" (v 13). As James will elaborate in verses 16–18, God is in the business of giving and doing good, not evil. So it simply isn't possible that He would attempt to bring us down spiritually. It is no more possible for God to tempt us than for Him to be tempted to do evil. Besides, why would He do such a thing? If He wanted to destroy us, He could simply destroy us.

The Real Source of Temptation

So where does temptation come from? At this point we might expect James to introduce the figure of Satan, but he doesn't. It's evident that James believes in an evil spirit being who works against our spiritual welfare by tempting us, since in 4.7 he urges us to "Resist the devil, and he will flee from you." This makes it all the more surprising that he doesn't bring up the devil in this context as the source of temptation. Why not?

James' goal here is to stress our personal responsibility in the matter of temptation and sin. While it's true that Satan is "the tempter" (1 Thess 3.5), a "murderer" and "the father of lies" (John 8.44), and our spiritual "adversary" (which is the meaning of his name in both Greek and Hebrew, 1 Pet 5.8), he couldn't do anything to move us to sin if we weren't complicit in the whole thing. That's the point James wants to make here: don't blame God; blame yourself when you sin. So in verses 14 and 15 James outlines the temptation process: our own desires "lure and entice" us; desire "conceives" and then "gives birth" to sin; sin becomes "fully grown"; and "death" results. Let's unpack that a bit.

First James describes the process of being "lured and enticed" by our desires. Our desires may not be sinful in themselves, but we are sometimes tempted to satisfy them in ways that are. In other cases we desire things that are sinful. For example, God gives us our sexual desires and also provides a God-ordained means for their satisfaction (a heterosexual marital union). Those same desires, however, can entice us to adultery or to homosexual activity, both of which are condemned by God. The language James uses ("lured and enticed") sounds like someone going fishing, only in this case we provide the bait that lures us toward our own destruction. It's a striking image: fish who lure themselves into being caught!

When does desire "conceive and give birth to sin"? Usually when we have entertained it for awhile. This has largely to do with our thoughts but also involves people with whom we associate and places we choose to go. In all of these ways we are encouraging our desire to "lure and entice" us. Temptations are bound to present themselves to us, but we don't have to allow them a place in our thoughts and lives. Entertaining them over a long period of time is asking for trouble. Most people don't sin at the first sight of temptation but usually only after thinking about it for awhile or being exposed repeatedly to the temptation. Eventually the desire "conceives and gives birth" when we commit the sin we've been thinking about. Left unchecked, such sin will become "fully grown," that is, it will come to dominate us and have a permanent place in our lives. When this happens, sin "brings forth death."

It isn't difficult to see the importance of wisdom in this scenario. We should be wise enough to avoid people and situations which tempt us and wise enough to keep our desires in check, realizing that the failure to do so leads inevitably to spiritual death. Not to do so is like riding a motorcycle going the wrong way down a busy highway while blindfolded; the results are inevitable.

God, the Giver of Good

Having made it clear where temptation comes from, James returns in verse 16 to the theme of God's goodness. Far from being the one who tempts us, God is the giver of "every good gift and every perfect gift." Notice that James urges the readers not to be deceived. About what? About the fact that God in no way tempts His people, but that we—not God—are the source of the problem. In verse 17 James identifies God, "the Father of lights," as the source of everything good. The Bible calls God "the Father of lights" only here, but it is most likely a reflection of the Genesis account of creation, which began with God decreeing, "Let there be light." As Lord of all creation, God is the "Father of lights," since He brought the sun, moon, and stars into being. But it is not as "Lord" that James here characterizes God but as "the Father." This not only points to Him as the source of the lights of the creation but also as our Father, the One who desires only our good and would never work to our harm. This truth forms the basis upon which we pray, according to Jesus in Luke 11.11–12. As is the case with any loving father, God longs to give good gifts— and *only* good gifts—to His children.

James adds to His portrait of God by saying, "with [Him] there is no variation or shadow due to change" (v 17). If it were not for this simple, foundational truth, prayer and life in general would be a precarious affair. How would we ever know what sort of mood God was in? Is He likely to hear and grant my request today, or is He having a bad day that will cause Him to become infuriated at my request? The constancy of God's nature is fundamental to our relationship to Him and also guarantees that He is out to do us no harm, ever, at any time.

Further evidence of God's goodness lies in the fact that He "brought us forth by the word of truth," which is apparently a reference to conversion and salvation. "The word of truth" is an apt expression to describe the gospel, since through this word we learn the truth about our lost status without Christ, the truth of what He has done to redeem us, and the glorious future He has prepared for us. Hearing, believing, and obeying this word of truth causes us to be "brought forth" (apparently a parallel to the imagery of being "born again" in John 3.5) as God's own children. Notice the contrast between what happens when we leave our desires unchecked ("sin *brings forth* death") and what God does for us ("he *brought us forth* by the word of truth"). And He has done this "of his own will," not because of anything we have done or have deserved but simply because He chose to do it. As a result we are "a kind of firstfruits of his creatures."

As I'm typing this, my computer refuses to recognize the word "firstfruits" (even though the term occurs in the ESV), so that probably means it needs some explanation. Israel was commanded to give the "first fruits" of their harvested crops, of newborn animals, and even of their children (who were redeemed with a monetary gift) in sacrifice to God (see Exod 13.11–16, Lev 23.9–14, Num 15.17–21, Deut 18.4–5), and these came to be known by the combination term "firstfruits." The idea is that firstfruits given to God show He has priority in our lives to the point that we commit to Him first, even before securing our own needs. It also means we trust Him fully that there will be "secondfruits" to follow. And, since the firstfruits are usually the best fruits (think of that first ripe tomato from the garden or the first peach from the tree), it demonstrates our conviction that He deserves the best we have. Calling Christians "firstfruits" therefore is a symbolic way of speaking of the devotion of our entire lives, that we belong to Him and therefore rightly offer God the best of all we are and have. In a similar way the prophets sometimes spoke of the entire nation of Israel as God's "firstfruits" among the nations; they were His chosen people, but one day all nations would come to worship God (Gen 3.15, Jer 2.3, Isa 42.6). Now, James says, believers in Christ are "firstfruits," because through us God wants to bring everyone to salvation.

A Plan for Wise Endurance

So what would James have you do when faced with trials severe enough to cause you to question the goodness of our Father? What is the course of wisdom?

1. Remember that God has a blessing in store for you at the end of your trials, the "crown of life" which He has promised to all who love Him.

2. Don't even entertain the possibility that God is somehow trying to bring you down spiritually by allowing this trial in your life. It isn't in His nature to do so. Trials are opportunities for growth and strength, which is why God allows them.

3. Accept responsibility for allowing yourself to be "lured and enticed" by your desires, realizing you may be setting in motion a dreadful process of temptation leading to sin leading to death, and only you can prevent this.

4. Continually acknowledge God as "the giver of every good and perfect gift." A God like that isn't going to do anything to bring you down; He will only lift you up.

5. Be confident every day of your life that God never changes and that His desire to give you good things is constant. You can count on it.

6. Give thanks to God daily for having saved you through "the word of truth" and make it your aim to live in accordance with that word.

7. Recognize the honor of being "a kind of firstfruits" of God's creatures and devote yourself to bringing glory to God for bestowing this great gift.

When you have the wisdom to respond to your trials in this manner, you will be truly "blessed" (v 12).

Great is Thy faithfulness, O God my Father,
There is no shadow of turning with Thee;
Thou changest not, Thy compassions, they fail not;
As Thou hast been Thou forever wilt be.

Thomas O. Chisholm, "Great Is Thy Faithfulness"

"But be doers of the word, and not hearers only, deceiving yourselves." (1.19–27)

SIX | *The Wisdom to Hear and Do*

As we've observed already, James may not quote his better-known brother all that frequently, but the letter reflects the teachings of Jesus throughout, and the three brief paragraphs on "hearing and doing the word" provide an obvious example. Jesus' Parable of the Sower (Matt 13.1–8) has been described as "a parable about all the parables," because it's about the way people respond to the word of the kingdom. The various soils in the parable represent different types of hearts and what happens when the message of the gospel lands on each. The point of the parable is not that some are able to hear the message more clearly (and more fruitfully) than others; rather, it demonstrates that some are simply more *willing* than others to let the word change them.

The climax of the parable comes at the end, when Jesus says, "He who has ears, let him hear." Our more contemporary way of putting it would be, "Listen up!" Jesus emphasizes that whether or not we hear what God has to say to us is a matter of choice. He has revealed Himself through His Son and through Scripture; the same revelations are available to all who hear or read the gospel. The question is, are we *wise enough* not only to hear but also to do God's word? Although James doesn't use the terms "wise" or "wisdom" in 1.19–27, it's clear he is still focusing on what wise living is, and no one who refuses to be changed by the word can be called wise. The kind of "hearing" that both Jesus and James talk about isn't just auditory reception; rather, it's "effectual hearing," hearing that actually changes us. It is hearing that leads to doing.

What does it take to hear in this sense? James 1.19–27 gives important guidelines.

Clearing the Ground

Every good gardener knows that the first step to a good harvest is clearing the ground of all the weeds, roots, and debris that might hinder growth. Since James is interested in the spiritual growth of his readers, that's what he addresses in 1.19–21. Every day we encounter all kinds of mental and spiritual clutter that keeps us from hearing God's word the way He wants us to and so hinders our spiritual growth. So it just has to go. What kind of clutter is it?

Talking rather than listening. James says we (all of us—"every person") should be "quick to hear" but "slow to speak" (v 19). Have you ever heard someone say something like this: "I know what the Bible says, but my God wouldn't condemn anyone for not believing in Him"? Or, "I don't think God would _____" (fill in the blank). "I just don't understand why God requires _____" (again, take your choice; there are lots of options). What's happening here is that people are speaking their own mind rather than trying to learn the mind of God. Result: They don't hear what God has to say.

I was checking into a hotel in London and a young bellman was showing me to my room. On the way up in the elevator he asked where I had been, and I told him to Ukraine for a mission trip. I was hoping this would give me an opportunity to talk to him about Christ, but once he heard what I'd been doing, he began to tell me all of his own views about God (none of which were even close to Scripture or had anything to do with Jesus) and continued to do so until we reached my room. I never got a chance to say much of anything other than "Uh-huh." It occurs to me that many folks are that way with God—talking so much about their own ideas that they never hear His.

When Stephen Hawking, the brilliant theoretical physicist, gives lectures, he has to compose them on a computer ahead of time because of his paralysis. Then he pushes a button and lets the machine do the talking for him. Following his lectures, he often entertains questions from the audience. Normally it takes ten to fifteen minutes for him to program a response to each question, and I have read that during the entire time there will be complete silence from the audience, because they are waiting to see what this great mind has to say. Clearly they are convinced Hawking is worth listening to. Shouldn't we be even more "quick to hear" what the Creator of the universe has to say than we are to hear the ideas of someone who can only theorize about what the Creator has done? But, in order to hear Him, we have to hold our tongues and listen. Acts 17.21 gives a telling description of the Athenians of Paul's day: "Now all the Athenians and the foreigners who lived there would spend their time in nothing except telling or hearing something new." Is it any wonder Paul opened his sermon to such a crowd by telling them they were worshiping that which they did not know (vv 22–23)?

We can't effectively hear God unless we cease speaking long enough to hear what He has to say.

Anger. Along with being quick to hear and slow to speak, James says we must be "slow to anger" in order to hear God. Some think James means we must put away our anger *toward one another*, and this is a plausible interpretation. However, it's difficult to see how the subject of being angry with one another fits in the context of what we must do in order to listen to God. It seems far more likely that James means we should be "slow to anger" in response to what we hear from God's word.

Remember the story of Cain and Abel in Genesis 4.1–7? Abel offered an acceptable sacrifice and Cain didn't. When God rejected his offering, Cain became angry rather than penitent, and ended up killing his brother out of resentment and jealousy. With such an extreme response, it's hard to believe he actually heard anything God said to him. His anger only led to greater sin. As James says, "the anger of man does not produce the righteousness that God requires" (v 20). It certainly didn't in Cain's case.

No one likes to be rebuked. But if you find God's word rebuking you (which is one of its inspired functions—2 Tim 3.16), you'd better be wise enough to listen.

Moral Uncleanness. Immoral attitudes and behaviors have a way of making us deaf to God. When uncleanness fills our lives, there's simply no room for God's word and usually little interest in it. James describes such uncleanness vividly as "filthiness and rampant wickedness" (v 21), and it just has to go if we're ever to hear what God has to say. This means we all need constant self-examination to see if there is any uncleanness within us and to pray that God will likewise do a "search and destroy" mission on the sinful things that may inhabit our lives.

> Search me, O God, and know my heart!
> Try me and know my thoughts!
> And see if there be any grievous way in me,
> and lead me in the way everlasting! (Psa 139.23–24)

Because such uncleanness makes us deaf to God, we simply have to "put [it] away"—i.e., get rid of it. And, it's necessary to guard what we allow into our consciousness through the media and other avenues as well. As Paul elaborates in Ephesians 5.1–11, we can't "imitate Christ" and "learn what pleases the Lord" while taking part in the "works of darkness."

Receiving the Seed

Notice the contrast between the first and second halves of verse 21. First we are to "put away all filthiness and rampant wickedness," then "receive with meekness the implanted word." It isn't enough just to get rid of the bad stuff; we have to replace it with the right stuff as well.

The word James uses for "receive" (*dechomai*) means in some contexts to "welcome" (see Col 4.10 and Heb 11.31 for example). It suggests a positive response to God's word, unlike the hard soil along the path in Jesus' parable. To "receive the word" means simply to let it in. In order to let it in, we must have plenty of exposure through reading, studying, and hearing the word expounded, so this "receiving" is an active and not a passive process. The receptive attitude is that of "meekness," the humility to acknowledge both our need and our trust in God's power to provide what we need.

When we receive the word, it becomes "implanted" in us and is "able to save [our] souls." So the decision to hear and receive the word is also a decision to live. The decision not to hear means choosing to die.

Doing What We Know

There is always the temptation spiritually to confuse knowing with doing. It's easy to think that, because we have heard or read what God says in Scripture, we have done all He desires of us. James doesn't want his readers even getting close to that error, so he warns them to "be doers of the word and not hearers only, deceiving yourselves" (v 22). Thinking we can become what God wants simply by knowing His word is like reading a book on exercise in order to get in shape. Know-how is important, but putting into practice what we know is vital. Jesus forcefully brought this point home as He concluded the Sermon on the Mount:

> Everyone who hears these words of mine and does them will be like a wise man who built his house on the rock. And the rain fell, and the floods came, and the winds blew and beat on that house, but it did not fall, because it had been founded on the rock. And everyone who hears these words of mine and does not do them will be like a foolish man who built his house on the sand. And the rain fell, and the floods came, and the winds blew and beat against that house, and it fell, and great was the fall of it. (Matt 7.24–27)

Not only is hearing but not doing a form of self-deception, it's also useless. James likens it to a man who looks at himself in the mirror, does nothing about what he sees, then goes away and forgets what he saw. (Can you imagine doing that in the morning when you first get up?) By contrast, the person who both looks (carefully, the Greek implies) and acts "will be blessed *in his doing*" (v 25). It's in living out the word of God that we find ourselves blessed, not just from knowing what's right and what isn't.

In verse 25 James speaks of God's word as "the perfect law, the law of liberty," and we need to ask why. Perhaps the following observations will help:

1. In 2.8 he uses the expression "the royal law" but then refers again to "the law of liberty" in 2.12. The "royal law," based on the context, is the law of loving your neighbor as yourself, while the "law of liberty" is most likely a description of the gospel message, what Paul calls "the law of Christ" in Galatians 6.2 and "the law of the Spirit of life" in Rom 8.2.

2. The expression "the law" in James 2.9–11 apparently refers to the Law of Moses itself.

3. In each case the term "law" refers to a manner in which God deals with His people, whether Israel (in the case of the Law of Moses) or the church ("the law of liberty," "law of Christ," etc.).

4. Remember that the Hebrew term *torah* doesn't mean "law" only in the sense of rules and regulations, since the word itself means "teaching," which obviously includes rules but also much more. It's everything God wants us to know about Himself and about how to live in order to make it through this world spiritually intact.

5. In the case of "the law of liberty," we have a law which sets us free rather than one which binds us, as the Law of Moses did due to our inability to keep it perfectly (see Gal 5.3 and Jas 2.10). Through the power of Jesus' blood, we are set free from sin in spite of our imperfections, so the gospel is a "law" which gives liberty.

6. However, even this "law" includes certain standards by which we are to live (as the letter of James itself makes clear), so when we look into it, we should resolve to change our behavior to meet God's standards. And, as James says, we should "persevere" in doing so rather than simply being different for a little while (such as the duration of a worship service).

7. The "law" which we have through Christ (the gospel) is "perfect" because it completes all that we need to have fellowship with God, and it is the "law of liberty" because it sets us free from our failure and condemnation.

Back to the idea of being blessed by doing. If you find yourself frustrated with your spirituality, not growing in God's service, and wondering why He doesn't bless you more, ask yourself, "Am I doing what I know?" Remember: we are "blessed in our doing." Otherwise, your knowledge is simply useless.

For Instance…

Being the ever-practical teacher that he is, James gives three specific examples of knowing and doing. He states the first one in the negative: "If anyone thinks he is religious and does not bridle his tongue but deceives his heart, this person's religion is worthless" (v 26). "Worthless" is about the worst thing that could be said about someone's religion, but James adamantly insists this is the case with those who fail to control their tongues. Again he states that such people are self-deceived, this time specifying that it is the "heart" that is deceived, and it is deceived by the loose-talker himself. People who have been in Christ for years yet still gossip and criticize one another fall into the category of the deceived. James has much more to say on the subject of the tongue and its misuse in chapters three and four, but it's already evident that he regards control of the tongue as a hallmark of a truly spiritual person.

His second example of putting the word into action involves taking care of people in need, specifically orphans and widows, two of the most helpless groups of his day. This should come as no surprise, since the Old Testament describes God as "Father of the fatherless and protector of widows" (Psa 68.5). Likewise Isaiah admonished Israel to "cease to do evil; learn to do good; seek justice, correct oppression; bring justice to the fatherless, plead the widow's cause" (Isa 1.16–17). James says specifically to "visit" orphans and widows in their affliction, but the verb *episkeptomai* means far more than simply "stop by to see how they're doing." It's from the same root as the word for "overseer" (sometimes translated "bishop"), an alternate term for elders or shepherds. (See the combination of these terms in 1 Pet 5.1–2, where the "elders" are told to "shepherd the flock of God…exercising oversight" [*episkeptomai*].) What James has in mind is taking care of the needs of orphans and widows, since by definition they had no one else to take care of them and in ancient societies were often destitute. Although some churches tend to think of such benevolence as a somewhat secondary activity to the church's real business of evangelism, it clearly was not so in James' mind. Rather it was (and is) another means of telling and demonstrating God's love and care. Such a practical religion is, in James' estimation, "pure and undefiled before God." It can't get much better than that.

Example number three concerns moral purity: "and to keep oneself unstained from the world" (v 27b). This is the other side of "pure and undefiled religion," to actively pursue doing good to those in need while at the same time avoiding the sin and confusion that "the world" (i.e., the world without God) constantly seeks to thrust upon us. It's so easy to become stained by this world's thinking and behavior, especially in its warped value system and ungodly attitudes. The more "stained" we become by worldly thinking and behavior, the less useful we are to God. An expensive shirt that becomes stained may still be worn for some things, but its usefulness is severely limited; so it is with our lives. Being stained by the world isn't always obvious. For example, it's commonplace among Christians to think it's okay to buy things we don't need simply because we can afford it. But that isn't a spiritual way to use the resources God has put in our care. This kind of thinking reflects the stain of a materialistic, self-centered world, and a believer who truly seeks God's kingdom first will put the teaching of Jesus into action rather than just paying lip-service to it while using the resources God provides for his or her own ends.

It isn't really that hard to *know* what God expects and requires of us. What's difficult is disciplining ourselves to *do* it by making the necessary changes in our lives. Here's where we need both wisdom and strength, but God promises to supply both. Hearing and doing the word—without doubt, that's the way to blessing.

I'll say yes, Lord, yes, to Your will and to Your way,
Yes, Lord, yes, I will trust You and obey;
When the Spirit speaks to me with my whole heart I'll agree
And my answer will be "Yes, Lord, "yes!"

Lynn Keesecker, "Yes, Lord, Yes"

*"My brothers, show no partiality as you hold the
faith in our Lord Jesus Christ."* (2.1–9)

SEVEN | *Polluted by Partiality*

As I pulled up to the intersection and stopped at the light, I couldn't
help but notice the woman standing on the median strip. She was
holding a sign, asking for donations, but what really got my attention was her shabby appearance. She was dirty and unkempt, and
her clothes were old and ragged. Since I'd been studying James
2.1–9, I wondered, "If she showed up at our church this Sunday
morning, what kind of reception would she receive?" I concluded
she almost certainly would receive a warm welcome, because we
have an open and accepting group of folks who are quick to put
strangers at ease, no matter who they are or how they look. But I
also found myself thinking that her reception among us might be
the exception and not the rule; in many churches she would probably be ignored—or worse.

James seems confident that a woman like the one I saw wouldn't
have gotten a proper welcome in the church(es) to whom he was
writing. In verse 6 he speaks in the past tense when he mentions
the dishonoring of the poor who came into their worship assemblies.
Apparently he knew that a great tragedy had already happened there.
Someone (perhaps many) had come to worship with them, only to
be dishonored by the church's inexplicably prejudiced behavior.

Two Different Men, Two Different Reactions

James 2.1–3 provides an example of James' mastery of painting a vividly memorable scene with only a few words. He describes a typical Sunday worship meeting attended by two atypical visitors. He prefaces his description with a blunt admonition against showing partiality while holding faith in Christ (v 1). The two are completely incompatible, since Christ died for all and to save all. How can His people now live out their faith discriminating against others based on their appearance? And appearance is what this scenario is all about.

The setting is a Christian "synagogue" or place of assembly. As we've already discussed, the use of the Greek *synagogue* suggests a Jewish Christian church and an early date for the letter, since most ancient Christians didn't normally refer to their meetings in this way. In fact, this is the only occurrence of the word in this sense in the entire New Testament. Early Christians quickly began to use the Greek term *ekklesia* ("church") to describe their meetings, in order to distinguish themselves from Jewish assemblies, especially among Gentile churches. Both terms emphasize the assembly or gathering itself more than the place.

Into this assembly come two men, both arriving at about the same time. Both are apparently strangers to this church, but on the surface at least, that's about all they have in common. James describes one as rich and the other as poor, with the sole determining factor being their appearance. The rich man is obviously (perhaps even ostentatiously) rich. He is wearing "fine (literally 'shining') clothing" which makes him stand out as a man of considerable means. Plus he is wearing a gold ring, not the norm in the ancient world as it is in our culture today, so another indicator of wealth. The poor man is the rich man's opposite in every way. For one thing, there is no mention of a ring at all. Poor people at that time didn't have them. And his clothing, in contrast to the classy attire of the rich man, is "shabby." To be more specific, James uses a word to describe the poor man's clothes that actually means "dirty" or even "filthy." This is important, I think, because most of us react differently to someone who is filthy than to someone who is merely shabby but clean. There is nothing attractive about this man; he is shabbily dressed and his clothing is offensively dirty. In appearance he is the rich man's opposite.

Based on nothing other than appearance, the two men receive quite opposite greetings once they enter. Church members "pay attention" (the first step toward a welcome) to the rich man and offer him a seat of honor in the assembly. But the treatment the poor man receives is as shabby as his clothing: he is told he can either stand and not sit at all or else sit on the floor. We might be tempted to think that James is merely exaggerating for effect, that surely no one would be so crass as to suggest that a visitor sit on the floor. But we should remember the wide disparity between rich and poor that existed in the ancient world and that often exists today and the harsh treatment which is standard in such cultures. Besides, how much difference is there between asking a dirty visitor to sit on the floor and merely ignoring him so that he doesn't know where to sit or even if he is welcome to sit at all?

It's a Sin!

Experts in the growth and functioning of churches have long observed that almost all churches think they're friendly. And most are—at least to each other. In most instances it's not easy for a newcomer to break into the circle and find a genuine welcome. This is a sad state of affairs, and churches should do whatever they can to correct it as quickly as possible. But what James describes goes even beyond this kind of indifference. The mistreatment of the poor is nothing short of sinful, and he doesn't hesitate to say so (v 9). How else will his readers know the seriousness of the situation and the urgency of correcting it? So James offers several reasons why he (and God!) finds such behavior so offensive.

First, showing partiality is entirely inconsistent with the Christian faith. It's true that Jesus at one point gave His disciples a "limited commission" to go only "to the lost sheep of the house of Israel" with the good news of the kingdom, and not to Gentiles or Samaritans (Matt 10.5–8). But this was a temporary measure designed to make the point that Jesus had come to fulfill all of God's promises to Israel by being the Messiah they had so long hoped for. This had to happen first before anyone else was privileged to hear the good news of the Savior. At the end of the Gospel Jesus expands the commission to include "all nations," and the rest of the New Testament makes it clear that this was the course the apostles followed, though not without divine prompting. When Peter went to the home of the man who would become the first known Gentile convert to Christianity, a Roman centurion named Cornelius, he declared, "Truly I understand that God shows no partiality, but in every nation anyone who fears him and does what is right is acceptable to him" (Acts 10.34–35). If even God doesn't show partiality, how can His people dare to do so? So James commands his readers to "show no partiality as you hold the faith in our Lord Jesus Christ, the Lord of glory" (2.1). J. B. Phillips paraphrased this verse this way: "Don't even attempt to combine snobbery with faith in our glorious Lord Jesus Christ." Jesus showed no partiality when He went to the Cross, and we have no right to do so.

Second, partiality involves judging by a false standard. James says when we judge people by their appearance, we "have made distinctions among [ourselves] and become judges with evil thoughts" (v 4). The New American Standard Bible says "judges with evil motives." The word for "partiality" means literally "to receive the face," to make judgments based on external factors such as appearance, social status, race, etc. Even God doesn't do this, as Samuel learned when he was sent to anoint Israel's second king. He looked at Jesse's eldest son and concluded on the basis of his looks that "surely the Lord's anointed [was] before him" (1 Sam 16.6). But Samuel was quickly informed that "the Lord sees not as man sees; man looks on the outward appearance, but the Lord looks on the heart" (16.7). We can't judge people's hearts, which is probably one reason we so often base our opinions of others on outward appearance. The danger in doing so is that our thoughts and motives are so often "evil," as James says. Are we accepting one person and rejecting another because one looks as if she or he might be of help to us or able to enhance us in some way whereas the other can't? Such thinking is both selfish and evil.

Third, such partiality is unacceptable because it's contrary to God's estimation of the poor. Verse 5 reminds us that God has "chosen those who are poor in the world to be rich in faith and heirs of the kingdom." What's James getting at in that statement? For one thing, the Bible says that God has a special place in His heart for the poor. Proverbs 14.31 says, "Whoever oppresses a poor man insults his Maker, but he who is generous to the needy honors him." The Law of Moses taught Israel repeatedly never to take advantage of the poor but to render help when needed (Deut 23.19–20, Exod 22.25–27, Lev 25.35–38). When Jesus attended the synagogue in His hometown of Nazareth, He proclaimed His messiahship by quoting the words of Isaiah 61.1, that He had been "anointed … to proclaim good news to the poor…to set at liberty those who are oppressed" (Luke 4.18). But there is another sense in which God has "chosen the poor." Think of all the times in Scripture when God has worked through the poor and the powerless in order to bring about the various stages of His kingdom. To cite just one example, the couple God chose to be the earthly parents of Jesus were not from the ruling or wealthy classes of Palestine but rather were of the Jewish laboring class. Our Lord Himself was placed in a feed trough for animals as His first bed, and His life was immediately in danger from the rich and powerful Jewish king. No wonder James tells "the lowly brother" to "boast in his exaltation" (1.9)! God loves the poor, and if we don't, we're not Godly.

Fourth, James argues against discriminating against the poor and showing favoritism toward the rich because of the particular situation of his oppressed readers. Since the rich were oppressing them and dragging them into court and blaspheming the name of Christ, what sense did it make to show partiality toward the rich (vv 6–7)? So the problem is two-fold: not only discrimination against the poor but also favoritism toward the rich. Both are wrong. We need to remind ourselves here that James is generalizing with his statements about rich and poor. Obviously not all rich people oppressed the church, as 1.10 demonstrates, and it would be naïve to think that all poor people are righteous. But the common experience of his readers was suffering abuse at the hands of the rich, so why cater to them when they decide to come to church? Far too often Christians show deference to rich people who visit their assemblies or express interest in membership because they assume these people, with their enhanced financial assets, can be of special help to the church. And they can be if they so choose. However, all too often the rich become problematic precisely because they expect others to cater to their desires, since it's what they're used to in other spheres of life. Of course, the idea isn't to ignore the rich but rather to treat everyone with equal dignity and respect. It's the only thing that makes any sense.

Finally, James says not to show partiality because it's just plain sinful (vv 8–9). Apparently James was aware that some of his readers had been attempting to justify their preferential behavior toward the rich by citing the law of loving your neighbor as yourself, which James here labels as "the royal law," both because of its importance (Matt 19.34–40) and because it was spoken by the King Himself. Their reasoning seems to have been that if Jesus taught us to love our neighbors as ourselves then there's nothing wrong in showing preference for our rich neighbors, even at the expense of our poor ones. But James counters that this isn't really fulfilling the royal law and that showing partiality in favor of the rich and at the expense of the poor is sinful. Period. They shouldn't try to explain it or make excuses for it; they need to repent of it.

What's the Connection?

We've been arguing all along that James isn't simply a hodge-podge of quasi-religious sayings but rather that the book follows a consistent theme (wisdom for the dispossessed) and that its various sections somehow connect together if we'll only look for the connections. In the case of this admonition against partiality, what is the connecting link between 1.27 and 2.1? In 1.27 James said not only to take care of orphans and widows (invariably poor in ancient times) but also to "keep oneself unstained from the world." It's at that point he begins his sermon against showing partiality, because showing partiality is nothing less than a clear indication that a person's thinking has become polluted by the world. Preferring the rich over the poor, even in Christian worship, is an accommodation to the worldly assessment of people: those who matter are rich (or at least middle-class), have some degree of power (at least a credit card), and are physically attractive (even if only because of their expensive clothing and fine jewelry).

It clearly isn't James' intention to offer a blanket condemnation of the culture in which he lived, nor should we do so with ours. There are always some things about our culture that are good, and we should readily acknowledge that. But when some of our cultural values are sick, God expects His people to recognize that and not be corrupted by them but rather to expose them for what they are. And a church which shows partiality toward those who come into its midst will never do that. Too many of our cultural values concern status symbols, money, and celebrity. And some of the most profane people in our society are some of the richest and most famous, and millions pay deference to them simply because they are so. The point of James 2.1–9 is that showing partiality is simply one symptom of a larger problem of Christians having bought into the world's value system without even realizing it. It takes wisdom to see this, and even more to avoid becoming guilty of it.

> *When my love to Christ grows weak,*
> *When for deeper faith I seek,*
> *Then in thought I go to Thee, Garden of Gethsemane!*
> *When my love for man grows weak,*
> *When for stronger faith I seek,*
> *Hill of Calvary! I go*
> *To thy scenes of fear and woe.*

John R. Wreford, "When My Love to Christ Grows Weak"

"For whoever keeps the whole law but fails in one point has become accountable for all if it." (2.10–13)

EIGHT | *Guilty on All Counts*

Did you hear about the man who emailed his boss that he wouldn't be coming to work on Monday morning? "The dog ate my car keys, and we're hitchhiking to the vet." Or how about the teenager who brought this note to school after several days' absence: "Please excuse Johnny for being absent January 28, 29, 30, 31, 32, and 33."

Ever since the time of Adam and Eve, we humans have displayed a remarkable capacity for making excuses. As soon as the first sin was committed and God called Adam to account for it, Adam blamed Eve—and, by extension, God Himself! "The woman *whom you gave* to be with me, she gave me fruit of the tree, and I ate" (Gn 3.12). How could God blame Adam? After all, God had set him up by putting this woman in the way. Remember what Moses said when God first told him to go Egypt and demand that Pharaoh let the Israelites go? He was full of excuses. "Who will I say sent me?" "The people won't believe me." "I'm not eloquent." And when God had answered every objection Moses just pleaded, "Oh, my Lord, please send someone else" (Exod 4.13). After Israel escaped from Egypt and were gathered at Mt. Sinai, Moses was delayed coming down from his meeting with God on the mountain. The people got restless and demanded that

Aaron, Moses' brother, make gods for them, assuming that Moses was dead and the whole exodus project was in jeopardy. Aaron melted down the gold supplied by the people and made a calf which he "fashioned …with a graving tool" (Exod 32.4). Later, when called on the carpet for this sin, Aaron declared, "So they gave it to me, and I threw it into the fire, and *out came this calf*" (Exod 32.24). In other words, "It just happened." Moses was not amused and neither was the Lord.

"Just Loving Our Neighbors!"

It appears from reading the entire section of James 2.1–13 that some of James' readers were making excuses about showing partiality to the rich who came into their worship assemblies. That seems to be the connection between the scenario James describes in verses 1–7 and what follows in verses 8–13. Notice the word "really" in verse 8. They claimed they were just doing what Jesus said, loving their neighbors as themselves. It just happened that they were loving their *rich* neighbors in a special way while mistreating their poor neighbors, but at least they were trying to do what "the royal law" said. Perhaps they were also attempting to justify themselves by saying, "Maybe we don't treat the poor as we should, but we keep other commandments well, so we should still be okay." But James wasn't buying it, because what they were "really" doing was committing sin (v 9) and were therefore "convicted by the law as transgressors." Ironically, they were appealing to the law as justification for their sinful behavior, but James says it was the law that was actually condemning—not justifying—them.

Then in verse 10 James says something that has bothered his readers ever since: "For whoever keeps the whole law but fails in one point has become accountable for all of it." The Revised Standard Version and the New International Version use the word "guilty" rather than "accountable." How can that be? How can breaking one law make someone guilty of breaking the *whole* law? It hardly seems right or fair.

The answer is, breaking any of God's commands means you have become a law-breaker. For example, a bank robber might never commit a murder, but isn't that person a law-breaker nevertheless? When we use the term "convicted felon," we don't mean the person so described has committed every crime that might be labeled a "felony" but only that he has put himself into that category by committing one of the crimes which the law characterizes as a "felony." So James' point is, breaking God's law is breaking God's law, and the person who does so "has become accountable for all if it." Paul says something comparable in Galatians 5.3: "I testify again to every man who accepts circumcision that he is obligated to keep the whole law." God's law is an all-or-nothing proposition. In making the covenant with Israel, God didn't ask them to sign on for just part of it. Likewise, under Christ we are committed to doing His will—all of it. If we break one part, we are guilty of all.

If this still troubles you, consider this: There is only one Law-Giver, and all of His laws are expressions of His will. Breaking even one means we have violated the will of the Law-Giver. James makes this point in verse 11. The same God who spoke one of the commandments spoke them all. So even if I'm not guilty of breaking each individual commandment, I am still "a transgressor of the law."

"Have Mercy!"

So James urges us to speak and act "as those who are to be judged under the law of liberty" (v 12). Although the gospel, which seems to be what James means here by "the law of liberty" (see also 1.25, where this same "law" is also described as "the perfect law"), sets us free from the bondage of the condemnation we deserve, we will nevertheless be judged under that law. That is, God expects us to live by what He has given us, and our failure to do so is an indication we haven't taken Him seriously. So, James concludes, "judgment is without mercy to one who has shown no mercy. Mercy triumphs over judgment" (v 13). His readers need to understand that failing to show mercy to the poor affects God's willingness to bestow mercy on them.

What we find troubling about all of this is the strong connection James assumes between the Christian and the law. After all, didn't Paul write, "Christ redeemed us from the curse of the law" (Gal 3.13) and, "You are not under law but under grace" (Rom 6.14)? So why all this talk about the law? Many contemporary readers find themselves wanting to cry "Foul!" upon reading James' words, yet isn't James as inspired as Paul? But what happens to the beloved doctrine of justification by grace "apart from law" when we take James' words at face value?

Maybe This Will Help

The subject of the Christian's relationship to the law is too large and complicated for me to fully expound in this format. So at the risk of over-simplifying, I want to offer some principles suggested by this text that should help us keep things in perspective as we struggle with this somewhat complex topic.

1. *There is no part of God's law that we are at liberty to take lightly.* The discussion in 2.8–10 shows clearly that it isn't just the subject of love we must be concerned about but *all* of what God has commanded. It helps to remember that the Hebrew word for "law" (*torah*) actually means "instruction." Recognizing this doesn't detract from the fact that God has spoken in the imperative, but it puts the concept of "law" in a bit different light. Rather than thinking of God's "law" as merely a sequence of "dos" and

"don'ts," the concept of *torah* helps us realize that through His
law God is instructing His people in the way He desires us to
live and in the manner that is in our best interest. In this light, it
becomes more obvious that we don't want to disregard anything
God has said. Jesus brought home this point forcefully in the
Sermon on the Mount:

> Do not think that I have come to abolish the Law or the Proph-
> ets; I have not come to abolish them but to fulfill them. For
> truly, I say to you, not an iota, not a dot, will pass from the Law
> until all is accomplished. Therefore whoever relaxes one of the
> least of these commandments and teaches others to do the same
> will be called least in the kingdom of heaven, but whoever does
> them and teaches them will be called great in the kingdom of
> heaven. For I tell you, unless your righteousness exceeds that of
> the scribes and Pharisees, you will never enter the kingdom of
> heaven. (Matt 5.17–20)

And in Matthew 23.23–24 He castigated the scribes and
Pharisees for tithing "mint and dill and cummin" while neglect-
ing what He called "the weightier matters of the law: justice and
mercy and faithfulness." These teachings make it clear that we
should think of "the law" in a seamless fashion as the totality of
the teaching that comes from God, what Peter Davids calls "the
unitary conception of the law."

Of course, parts of God's law are not intended for Christians.
For example, the New Testament (especially Hebrews) makes it
clear that because of Jesus' sacrifice on the cross, there is no longer
any point to the animal and other sacrifices taught in the Old Testament. Still, we don't disregard these commandments but rather
learn from them, as Hebrews clearly demonstrates. They are a
"shadow" of what Jesus accomplished and understanding them

helps us appreciate His sacrifice more fully. And even though we are "under grace" and not law, the Scriptures give specific laws that Christians are obligated to keep. Think of what are sometimes called the "practical sections" of Paul's letters, where, after expounding the theological truths that undergird Christian living, he gives specific instructions on how to put these principles into practice. (The clear breaks between Ephesians 1–3 and 4–6 and Romans 1–11 and 12–16 are good examples of this indicative/imperative structure.) Even James' brief letter contains no fewer than 54 imperatives, explicit commands which the writer clearly expected his readers to obey.

So we should be careful about thinking that because we are under grace and not law that we have no "laws" to obey or that we are at liberty to disregard anything God has said.

2. *We can't use one Scripture to cancel out another.* James' readers were evidently using the love command to cancel out the teaching against showing partiality. While this might seem somewhat unlikely to us, it actually happens all the time. For example, how often have you heard someone reply in the context of a discussion of morality, "Judge not that you be not judged!" (Matt 7.1)? Jesus did teach that, but the statement occurs in the context of not judging others harshly or unfairly. It was never meant to say that it's wrong to characterize someone's immoral behavior as wrong! (Why is it that so many non-believers know only that one verse?) So here's a case of using one Scripture as a kind of trump card to cancel out others. Likewise, in discussions of how to be saved, many cling tenaciously to the great promise contained in John 3.16 that "whoever believes in him should not perish but have eternal life." The word "believes" is usually taken to mean some sort of internal process of conviction separate and apart from any outward expression of faith, any act of obedience. Yet there are

texts such as Acts 2.38 which emphasize the role of repentance and baptism in becoming a Christian. While it may be more attractive and comforting to think of "just believing," that isn't all God has to say on this subject.

So it isn't legitimate to focus only on one text and ignore the rest. Such a practice is extremely disrespectful of God's word. Obviously, based on the principle of taking all of God's word seriously, our only option is to examine all of the Scriptures and do our best to obey.

3. *Every one of us is a law-breaker.* James could hardly be clearer on this point than in verse 10: break one command and you're "guilty on all counts." This leads to two important conclusions.

First, it's a powerful reminder that we can never save ourselves through law-keeping. As Paul emphasizes, failure is inevitable in this department, which is the "curse of the law"—not the law itself but the fact of our inability to keep it perfectly so that it can function as an instrument of salvation. (Read Gal 3.10–14 carefully if you're unsure on this point.) Nothing we do can accrue sufficient merit before God so that He "owes" us heaven. We can't give enough, attend enough, serve enough, sacrifice enough, or pray enough to take away the guilt of our own sins.

Second, it brings us face to face with the reality that we're saved by God's grace, or we aren't saved at all. Paul again expands this thought in Ephesians 2.1–10. Without Christ, he says, we were "dead in our trespasses and sins," but now we are alive because of God's grace given through Jesus. This can only be God's free gift to us, not something we "achieve" for ourselves. How could we, who are all law-breakers, ever find salvation any other way? No wonder James, in thinking along these same lines, comes up with the expression "the law of liberty," since we are freed from the requirement to be perfect.

So don't spend your life trying to do the impossible; put your trust in Jesus and the power of His sacrifice to save you. As a law-breaker, you have no other hope.

4. *Even though we are "saved by grace," we are "judged by law."* This concept is so far outside the box for many that we truly need God's wisdom in order to grasp it and to grasp just how important it is. Look carefully at verses 12 and 13. James says to "speak and act" as those who are to be judged under the law of liberty, and then says that judgment is without mercy to those who refuse to show mercy. There's nothing new about this, because James has already insisted we are to be "doers of the word and not hearers only" (1.22) and we are deceived if we think otherwise. His definition of "pure and undefiled" religion is what we do—taking care of orphans and widows and keeping ourselves unstained from the world, along with curbing our venomous tongues (1.26–27).

James is far from alone in this outlook. Jesus said He will judge on the basis of whether or not those claiming to be His followers fed the hungry, clothed the naked, and cared for the sick and imprisoned (Matt 25.31–46). To do so leads to life; not to do so leads to condemnation in a place "prepared for the devil and his angels." Paul told the Corinthians that judgment is certain, "For we must all appear before the judgment seat of Christ," and that it is based on our works because each of us will "receive what is due for what he has done in the body, whether good or evil" (2 Cor 5.10).

But how can this be so without cancelling out the concept of grace? Because our actions show whether we've truly accepted God's grace or have spurned it. Sometimes our behavior shows we don't even comprehend grace. There is no more powerful illustration of this than Jesus' parable of the unmerciful servant (Matt 18.23–35), a story in which a man who had been forgiven something comparable to the national debt then refused to forgive a fellow-servant who owed him a few months' wages. The problem? He didn't at all grasp the blessing of forgiveness or else he would have gladly passed it on to someone else. After announcing the condemnation of the unmerciful servant, Jesus concludes that parable by saying, "So also my heavenly Father will do to every one of you, if you do not forgive your brother from your heart" (v 35). Does our forgiveness of others "earn" our own forgiveness from God? Of course not. It does, however, show whether or not we even comprehend what God has done for us. Refusal to forgive demonstrates that we haven't comprehended it. In 2.13 James brings home his point forcefully: "For judgment is without mercy to one who has shown no mercy. Mercy triumphs over judgment." We could think of this as Jesus' "beatitude" of Matthew 5.7 stated in the negative: "Blessed are the merciful, for they shall receive mercy."

Are we saved by grace? Yes, and only by grace, because we could never keep enough laws to erase the guilt of our sins. But if we are saved, it will be evident in our behavior, especially in our willingness to extend mercy to others.

Going back to the business of showing partiality, James says, "No excuses. Apply God's law of love equally to all and do what He does—show no partiality. Rather, extend mercy to all, because that's what we all want and desperately need." Those who are wise will take heed.

Merciful God and Father, Loving us like no other,
Hear our prayer, the cry of our hearts, as we come to You.
We acknowledge our transgressions, we confess to You our sins;
Show us mercy and compassion, touch our lives with Your healing grace again.
Release us from the past as we seek Your face.
Wash us free at last; we receive Your love, we receive Your healing grace.

John Chisum and Gary Sadler, "Healing Grace"

"So also faith by itself, if it does not have works, is dead." (2.14–26)

NINE | *A Faith that* Does

One of the most vivid scenes in the Book of Acts is in 26.24–29 when Paul made his defense before the Jewish king Herod Agrippa II and Porcius Festus, the Roman governor of Judea. As Paul related his Damascus Road vision of the risen Christ, Festus accused him of being insane. At that point Paul directed his comments specifically to the king, challenging him to declare whether or not he, as a Jew, believed the words of the Prophets:

> "King Agrippa, do you believe the prophets? I know that you believe." And Agrippa said to Paul, "In a short time would you persuade me to be a Christian?" And Paul said, "Whether short or long, I would to God that not only you but also all who hear me this day might become such as I am—except for these chains."

Clearly Agrippa did believe what the prophets had written, and he may have even been somewhat persuaded by the forcefulness of Paul's words. But he didn't *do* anything about it, in spite of Paul's impassioned plea.

And James says, "Be *doers* of the word, and not hearers only, deceiving yourselves" (1.22). Knowing is not doing. Information is not salvation. Cognizance is not obedience. Agreement with God's will is not alignment with God's will.

"What Good Is It?"

In 2.14–26 James puts the "doing the word" principle another way: "Faith without works is dead." That is, apart from actions, no matter how strongly one might believe, faith is utterly useless. We might ask why James takes off in this direction at this point in the letter. It probably has to do with the problem of partiality addressed in 2.1–7 and his readers' tendency to make excuses for it (2.8–13). They know it's wrong to favor the rich and dishonor the poor, but they do it anyway. So James asks, "Of what earthly use is that?"

At issue here is the nature of a faith that saves. The question isn't simply about opinions but about salvation, as verse 14 makes clear. Saving faith is not faith that knows what's right but doesn't do it. It isn't something that occurs only within our minds or our hearts. Unfortunately, this is what many people mean when they speak of "salvation by faith alone." They're referring to an internal reality with no external actions to accompany it. As a result, they believe you *can* have saving faith without works, what is sometimes more accurately called "belief only." James, on the other hand, argues that saving faith both believes and acts on that belief.

This confusion goes back at least as far as the Protestant Reformation, when Martin Luther and others argued for salvation by *sola fide* ("faith alone"). They were contending against the Roman Catholic Church's teaching that salvation comes through the performance of a series of works prescribed by the church. As the result of this controversy, "faith" came to be defined as that which is entirely internal; anything one *does* falls into the category of "works." This was and continues to be an unfortunate dichotomy, not only because it confuses the whole issue of what it takes to be saved, but also because it badly misses the point James is making.

Some Clarification, Please!

So what is James' point? Obviously, that faith cannot be merely internal; it must be a faith that acts as well as believes. In James' unforgettable language, an internal-only faith is "dead" (vv 17, 26) and "useless" (v 20). These terms are not all that different and point to the same reality: a dead faith *is* a useless faith. But just in case we missed the implications of this language, James puts it even more bluntly in verse 24: "You see that a person is justified by works and not by faith alone." (By the way, this is the only place in the entire Bible where the phrase "faith alone" occurs, and James denies that such a faith can save anyone.)

To be sure we don't miss his point, James offers a sequence of five illustrations which demonstrate his thesis that only an active faith is a saving faith.

Illustration number one is the case of a needy brother or sister (vv 15–17). It's one thing to see the plight of someone in need and even feel some pain over their circumstances, but it's an entirely different matter to give them what they need. All of our sympathy and good wishes won't put a coat on anyone's back or fill her stomach. Just as our emotions and cheery words are lifeless in meeting another person's need, so also "faith by itself, if it does not have works, is dead." The feelings are fine and the kind words will be appreciated, but only if they are backed up by action. Otherwise they're lifeless and cruel.

Next James makes a somewhat surprising comparison. In response to someone who might claim to be a "faith specialist" while others are "works specialists," James challenges that person to demonstrate his faith "apart from your works." How would you do that? Answer: You can't. James then offers the correct perspective by saying, "I will show you my faith by my works" (v 18). Taking that further, he congratulates the person for having some degree of faith but then says, "Even the demons believe—and shudder!" James obviously has in mind those occasions when Jesus encountered demon-possessed people and the demons expressed their fear of Him (Mark 1.23–24, 5.7, etc.), fully realizing that He had absolute authority over them and could destroy them if He chose to do so. Yet the faith of demons is a dead faith because it changes nothing. Demons may tremble at the sound of Jesus' name, but they don't fall down to worship and serve Him. We should bear in mind that James isn't intending to say that any of his readers are demonic in nature (although some of their behavior certainly was; see 3.15), but rather that their supposed faith, being devoid of works, is no more productive than that of the demons.

James' third illustration of faith and works is perhaps his most intriguing one, because he, like Paul in Galatians and Romans, cites Abraham as *the* example of genuine faith, but his point is not the same as Paul's (2.20–23). In verse 20 he prepares his readers for an example that he must have felt sure they couldn't deny, even going so far as to call anyone who would dissent from his view "you foolish person." His prime example of a working faith (*vs.* a workless one) is Abraham's offering of Isaac (Gen 22). God instructed Abraham to sacrifice Isaac, "your only son," in spite of His promise that Abraham would, through Isaac, become the father of a great nation. What a perplexing circumstance this must have been for Abraham! On the one hand he had God's promise of numerous descendants, but on the other hand he was instructed to kill the one who was the key to the fulfillment of that promise. Genesis records that he dutifully went up on the mountain with his son and the wood for the offering, but his hand was stayed at the last moment, and the Lord said (via His angel),

> By myself I have sworn, declares the Lord, because you have done this and have not withheld your son, your only son, I will

surely bless you, and I will surely multiply your offspring as the stars of heaven and as the sand that is on the seashore. And your offspring shall possess the gate of his enemies, and in your offspring shall the nations of the earth be blessed, because you have obeyed my voice (Gen 22.16–18).

For any believing Jew this should be compelling proof that "faith without works is dead," for God blessed Abraham because of his obedience, not because of his inner convictions. James further elaborates, pointing out that faith was "active along with his works, and faith was completed by works," which fulfilled the Scripture, "Abraham *believed* God, and it was counted to him as righteousness" (vv 22–23). The quotation from Genesis 15.6 in conjunction with Genesis 22.16–18 shows that "faith" does not mean something internal only. James states his conclusion in verse 24: "You see that a person is justified by works and not by faith alone."

What makes James' statement so interesting is that Paul uses the same person, Abraham, and the same Scriptures, Genesis 22.16–18 and 15.6, to say that Abraham was justified by faith and *not* by works. James even uses Paul's customary word for being put right with God ("justified") in respect to Abraham, only he says the opposite of what Paul says: "Was not Abraham our father *justified by works* when he offered up his son Isaac on the altar?" I'll discuss this more in the next section.

James' fourth illustration likewise centers around an Old Testament character, Rahab the prostitute. Joshua 2 records her story of hiding the Israelite spies during their conquest of Canaan, and Hebrews 11.31 says she did so "by faith." Although not an Israelite, Rahab was convinced that Israel's God would deliver her city (Jericho) into Israelite hands, so she hid the spies on condition that when they invaded the city, they would spare her and her family. One has to wonder if there were not other Canaanites in Jericho who had the same conviction but did nothing about it. Because Rahab both believed and acted, James says she was "justified by works."

The final illustration of the faith-without-works-is-dead principle is perhaps the simplest and most graphic: "For as the body apart from the spirit is dead, so also faith apart from works is dead" (v 26). A workless faith is just like a body whose spirit has departed: dead. Not a pretty picture, but we get the point.

James vs. Paul?

Students of both James and Paul have had a variety of interesting responses to these writers' use of the story of Abraham and the quotations from Genesis. Some suggest that the two are hopelessly in conflict, that Paul believed in salvation by faith alone and James believed in salvation by works. To these people the two claims are hopelessly irreconcilable. Others suggest that perhaps James merely misunderstood Paul, that he didn't really believe in the kind of hard-core works-righteousness he seems to be espousing, but rather is over-stating his case in response to what he (erroneously) thought Paul was saying. Neither of these conclusions is necessary, nor is either of them particularly helpful.

While James didn't misunderstand Paul, it may well be that others did, and James was aware of this as he wrote. One reason for dating James in the AD 50s or later is that his letter seems to reflect a knowledge of Paul's teachings, and Paul began his letter-writing career in the late 40s. Dating James in the 50s allows time for Paul's teachings (if not the letters themselves) to have spread sufficiently so that James' readers would have been aware of them. It isn't at all surprising that some of the first readers of James would have misunderstood Paul, since Paul himself was aware of distortions of his teachings (see Rom 3.1–8, 6.1–3).

In the case of James' readers, what might that misunderstanding have been? Simply this, that Paul's insistence on justification by faith apart from works was understood as justification by a workless faith, an internal-only faith, something neither Paul nor James believed. It is evident from Romans 2.6–11, 2 Corinthians 5.9–10, and elsewhere that Paul believed exactly as did James: faith without works is dead. So why the apparent conflict between Paul and James 2.14–26?

James and Paul are actually responding to two different questions, both having to do with the nature of faith. For Paul the question is, must people live by the Law of Moses and be circumcised in order to be saved? Do they need both faith in Christ and obedience to the Law of Moses? Paul's answer is an emphatic "No"—they don't need Christ plus anything. The sacrifice of Jesus, not our ability to keep the law, provides the power for salvation. In the context of this "justification by faith," however, there must certainly be obedience to the commands of God as a faithful response to what God has done in Christ. For James the question is quite different: Can we be saved by a faith that is purely internal and does nothing? James' response is an equally emphatic "No"—faith must be active or else it is completely useless. Neither James nor Paul believed people could save themselves by their good deeds (see Js 2.10), and neither believed that a belief-only faith could save anyone. In this respect the writings of both men are fully in keeping with the teachings of Jesus Himself, as expressed in the conclusion of the Sermon on the Mount (Matt 7.21–27). Only the faith of the one who "hears these words of mine and does them" leads to salvation.

Real faith, saving faith, living faith is an *active* faith, a faith that *does,* not merely a faith that *agrees.* Faith becomes saving faith only when our convictions compel us to obey and to serve. Otherwise our faith is dead.

Implications

The principle that saving faith is a faith that works has some rather obvious applications. First, for those of us who are already committed to following Jesus, we need to understand that unless we practice what we claim to believe, our faith is worthless. Worse, it makes a mockery of the name of Christ. Daily the name of Christ is dragged through the mud of scandal brought on by "believers" who make loud protestations of their faith (much as did some of James' first readers—2.14, 18) yet do nothing or do the opposite of what Christians should do. Satan wins no greater victory than to lull us into the deception of hearing but not doing, thus creating a lifeless church that will never have a positive impact on the world.

Second, there is a no less important implication for those who are not followers of Christ. Many know the gospel story and perhaps even agree that Jesus is God's Son and our Savior but have never been moved to repent and be baptized as Scripture teaches (Acts 2.36–38, 22.16). If you fall into this category, don't be deceived into thinking you can be saved simply by arriving at a particular opinion about Jesus or even by a profession of faith that never goes any further than to profess. Jesus isn't a political candidate who is looking for your vote. He's your Savior who is looking for disciples, people who will step up and say without hesitation, "I believe" as well as "I'll obey."

If faith doesn't lead you to obedience, it remains dead and useless. It's the kind of faith that Agrippa had and which the demons have, but it isn't saving faith. There's no wisdom in seeing ourselves as genuine believers if all we have is a lifeless faith devoid of action.

When we walk with the Lord in the light of His Word,
What a glory He sheds on our way!
While we do His good will, He abides with us still,

And with all who will trust and obey.
Trust and obey, for there's no other way
To be happy in Jesus, but to trust and obey.

J.H. Sammis, "Trust and Obey"

"And the tongue is a fire, a world of unrighteousness." (3.1–12)

TEN | *Untamed Fire*

James 3 begins with what seems at first like a rather abrupt shift in topic: "Not many of you should become teachers, my brothers, for you know that we who teach will be judged with greater strictness." Then, just when we're expecting him to give some sort of workshop on teaching, he begins to discuss how easily we sin through the avenue of speech. We have to wonder what all of this has to do (if anything) with the discussion of faith and works that ends chapter 2. Some would say, nothing at all.

But here's a likely chain of thought: James was aware of some who were teaching erroneously concerning the nature of saving faith, as indicated in 2.14–26. He seems to have specific arguments in mind that these people have made (v 18) and refers to the one who fails to see his point as "you foolish person" (v 20). The warning against inappropriately becoming teachers, then, would likely refer to these people. They not only misunderstand the nature of saving faith but want to teach their misunderstanding to others also. That being the case, it isn't hard to see why James launches into a discussion of the tongue and its misuse. After all, the tongue (symbolic of the speech produced by it) is the teacher's primary tool. So once again, there is a logical consistency to James' topics.

It Isn't Funny

Because we're so prone to getting into trouble via the avenue of the tongue, we generally make lots of jokes about it, and some of the situations we get ourselves into do seem funny. But there is a darker side to the misuse of the tongue that James cautions us not to overlook.

James says "we who teach shall be judged with greater strictness." Why? Because teachers generally have a wider sphere of influence than do others, and because we teach things that impact eternity. So we need to be very careful about what we teach. Proverbs 18.21 reminds us that "Death and life are in the power of the tongue." Our words, particularly in teaching the gospel of Christ, can impart life, whereas deceptive or false words can lead others to death. The tongue contains an awesome power indeed. No wonder Jesus warned, "I tell you, on the day of judgment people will give account for every careless word they speak, for by your words you will be justified, and by your words you will be condemned" (Matt 12.36–37).

That being the case, it seems that church leaders would do well to review their practices of recruiting teachers. We're often desperate to find teachers to fill slots in our classrooms, to the point that sometimes the only requirement for being a teacher is a willingness to show up. As a result, we may be placing people in spiritual jeopardy, both by putting unqualified people in the role of teachers as well as by exposing the church to their false or inadequate teachings. Paul says in Romans 12.7 that teaching is a "gift" bestowed by God on some but not on others, and we would do well to ask if the people we are encouraging to teach display any signs of having (or developing) that gift. What do our prospective teachers believe? Do they have an adequate grasp of the gospel and the ability to explain it? Are they careful and diligent students of Scripture so that they have substantive knowledge to impart? Do their lives reflect the reality of what we expect them to teach so that they can serve not only as instructors but also as examples to those who hear them? With James' words of warning ringing in our ears, we dare not be casual in our approach to teaching in the body of Christ.

So although James doesn't use the word "power" in these verses, this section is very much concerned with the power of the tongue, a power we dare not underestimate. What makes it so powerful?

Hard to Control

After his warning about teaching, James makes a rather startling statement: "For we all stumble in many ways, and if anyone does not stumble in what he says, he is a perfect man, able also to bridle his whole body" (v 2). According to James, control of the tongue is the last great untamed frontier of self-control, so much so that he describes anyone who achieves this feat as "perfect." Obviously James doesn't mean "sinless," because no one measures up to that standard. On the other hand, we can attain a kind of "perfection" in the sense of completeness or wholeness. So it isn't impossible that a person could be so in control of his tongue that he could be described as having complete control of himself. It's rare, but it does happen. Such a person is "able to bridle his whole body." The reference to a "bridle" anticipates the idea of a horse's bit in the next verse. For now James applies this imagery to the person who has complete mastery over his tongue.

One reason why the tongue is so hard to control is that there are so many ways we can use it to mess up. James' letter is filled with references to such verbal errors. Some who are tempted say, "I am tempted by God," which James explains isn't even possible (1.13). In other instances we are not as "slow to speak" as we ought to be (1.19). The "bridle" imagery occurs earlier in 1.26 to describe the person who thinks he is religious (and thereby accepted by God) but fails to "bridle his tongue" and so is deceived. Likewise the tongue has a role in how believers speak to visitors in their worship assemblies and whether they treat them respectfully or not (2.3). The rich who were oppressing James' readers sinned with their tongues by blaspheming God (2.7). Others declared they had faith even in the absence of works (2.14, 18) and sinned with their tongues by verbally comforting those in need while refusing to do anything to help them (2.16). In the midst of congregational squabbles, believers would sometimes "speak evil of one another" (4.11) and grumble against one another (5.9), while others spoke rashly of their business plans that didn't include God (4.13). Still others were guilty of using oaths to reinforce their words and as a result fell under condemnation (5.12). Indeed, "we all stumble in many ways," and many of those ways involve our tongues.

The tongue has the power to do good as well as evil, but James doesn't say much about that. His primary concern is to defuse the hostilities that were arising among his readers, not to give a complete catalogue of what can be accomplished with the tongue. In fact, 3.1 is the beginning of a section of the letter which continues all the way through 4.12, in which James deals with the problem of quarreling among Christians. So as a matter of practicality, it's the misuse of the tongue that is so much of a pandemic in the human race. But it doesn't have to be that way, and James offers a stern corrective to the problem, at least among believers.

Small Package, Huge Effect

Not only is the tongue hard to control, but its power is out of proportion to its size, which is the primary emphasis of verses 3–5. To make this point James uses three illustrations: bits in the mouths of horses, the rudders which guide great ships, and a small flame incinerating a great forest. The bit, small as it is, enables the rider to control the body of an animal that is far larger than not only its bit but than its rider as well. A ship's rudder determines the direction the vessel will go, even though the ship is many times larger than the rudder. And it only takes a spark to ignite a fire that can consume an entire forest. If you've ever witnessed the damage caused by a rumor, you get James' point. One person can make the slightest remark, maybe not even an accusation but only an innuendo, and the damage is set in motion. By the time the comment is repeated to who-knows-how-many others, someone's reputation may be in ashes, friendships are no more, and the flames of strife can engulf an entire church. If one is going to handle dynamite, he had best be aware of its power.

By the way, none of James' three illustrations is unique to him. Ancient Hellenistic writers often spoke of the bit, rudder, and fire examples as illustrations of the tongue's disproportionate power. This is a potent reminder that the problem of tongue-control cuts across all lines of nationality, religion, culture, and time.

James' point could hardly be clearer: The tongue may be a small part of your body, but how you use it can make or break your whole life.

Set On Fire By Hell

The reference to "fire" in verse 5 sends James off in a slightly different direction in his discussion of the tongue. Starting in verse 6 his words take on an even darker tone as he says the tongue itself "is a fire, a world of unrighteousness." The latter part of the verse contains something of a word-play, as James says the tongue is "set among our members, staining the whole body." In the first instance we would think of the physical tongue and its negative effects on our lives ("staining the whole body"). But James likely has something else in mind: the effect of the tongue on "the body of Christ," the church (see Eph 1.23, 1 Cor 12.12–

13, 27–28, etc.), since the context shows he is clearly dealing with circumstances of strife in the church (4.1), much of which is fueled by words.

But it's the source of that fire that deeply concerns James. The tongue not only sets "on fire the entire course of life" (i.e., potentially ruins the life of the individual and possibly of the church also), but it is "set on fire by hell." Just a few verses later James will speak of a kind of "wisdom" that is not heavenly but "demonic" (v 15). Clearly he believed that Satanic forces inspire both the abuse of the tongue and the use of destructive "wisdom" to disrupt the peace of the church. As evidence of this, James refers to the fact that all sorts of animals can be and have been tamed by humans, but the tongue remains a perpetual challenge. We should not understand "tamed" here to equal "domesticated." No one has ever harnessed whales for transportation or made pets out of hippos. Still, these can be dominated and controlled (even if only through death) by humans, but not so the tongue. It remains a constant source of trouble, "a restless evil, full of deadly poison." Again, James will not allow us to dismiss lightly the effects of the misuse of the tongue. It kills, often indiscriminately.

In addition to its other devastating effects, the tongue also is a source of hypocrisy, as expressed in verses 9–10. The same tongue with which we sing "How Great Thou Art" on Sunday morning can be used to pronounce curses on a brother or sister once the "Amen" has been said. In the first instance we praise God and in the second we curse those made in God's image so that both blessing and cursing come out of the same mouth. James makes an emphatic appeal to rectify this incongruity by saying, "My brothers, these things ought not to be so." The use of the term "brothers" to speak inclusively of the whole church stresses how out of place such misuse of the tongue is.

Mind Your Tongue!

Given the seriousness of the misuse of our tongues, here are some simple and practical suggestions:

1. *Be careful what you say.* Before you speak words that have the potential to do harm, ask yourself, "Is what I'm about to say really true?" "Does it need to be said, or am I just eager to say it?" And, "Is it likely to do good or to do harm?" Answering these honestly will go a long way toward helping you decide when to speak and when to hold your tongue.

2. *Be careful how you say it.* "A soft answer turns away wrath, but a harsh word stirs up anger" (Prov 15.1). Sometimes we have to disagree with folks or perhaps offer constructive criticism or maybe even rebuke. In those cases, do it with love, or don't do it at all.

3. *Be careful to whom you say it.* If something you're about to say is negative, it probably doesn't need to be said to very many. If it's about someone else, say it to them. Recognize that some people simply can't be trusted not to tell everything they hear, so don't tell them what you know (or suspect).

4. *If you're not sure you ought to say something, don't say it.* That moment of hesitation that crosses your mind may well be a warning from your conscience. Listen!

If there's any part of our lives in which we all need wisdom, it's in the use of our tongues. So seek God's wisdom before you speak, or don't speak at all.

Angry words! O let them never From my tongue unbridled slip;
May the heart's best impulse ever Check them ere they soil the lip.
Love is much too pure and holy, Friendship is too sacred far,
For a moment's reckless folly Thus to desolate and mar.
"Love one another," thus saith the Savior;
Children, obey the Father's blest command.

"Love One Another"

*"And a harvest of righteousness is sown in peace
by those who make peace." (3.13–18)*

1/18/2015

ELEVEN | *The Wisdom that Leads to Peace
(and the One that Doesn't)*

In the little letter of 3 John, the aged apostle immortalizes two
people about whom we know nothing other than what he tells
us. One is Gaius, the "beloved" friend to whom the letter is addressed. John pays him the high compliment of praying that his
physical health may match that of his spirit (v 2) and commends
him for giving help to those engaged in the spread of the gospel.
Clearly, Gaius was a good man, devoted to the gospel, and committed to the service of Christ.

But all was not well in the church where Gaius served, because
there was a man of opposite nature, Diotrephes, whose name has
become synonymous with self-serving ambition. There are only
two verses about him (vv 9–10), but they speak volumes as to his
negative character and show that he posed a contrast to Gaius in
every way. He refused to acknowledge the authority of the apostles and those sent by them and spoke against them instead. He
tried to undermine the good works of others, especially of people
such as Gaius who wanted to welcome traveling evangelists into
their homes and give them aid. And he wanted to "de-church"
everyone who disagreed with him. No wonder John follows his

comments about Diotrephes by encouraging Gaius not to "imitate evil but imitate good" (v 11).

Diotrephes in James?

You may be wondering, what does Diotrephes have to do with James? A great deal actually, because he embodies the kind of pseudo-wisdom James describes in 3.13–18. Since James focuses so much attention on the subject of godly wisdom, it isn't surprising that he describes its opposite: that which sometimes passes for wisdom but which is really anything but that. Apparently there were some "Diotrepheses" in the church or churches to whom James first wrote, perhaps the teachers-who-shouldn't-be in 3.1. This seems all the more likely since the section on false wisdom immediately follows the discussion of teachers who misuse their tongues. The details of this problem are far from clear, but it's apparent that someone is bent on having things their way at church rather than seeking the good of the whole body. Verse 13 may provide a clue that an unhealthy desire to teach is indeed the source of strife when we notice the connection between it and 2.18. Someone was teaching the possibility of genuine faith apart from works, and James challenged them to "show me your faith apart from your works, and I will show you my faith by my works." Now in 3.13 he says the "wise and understanding" person will "show his works in the meekness of wisdom." It's hard to think there isn't a connection between the wrong teaching (2.18–26), the wrong desire to teach (3.1), and the false wisdom that obviously isn't from above (3.13).

Remember that the larger context of 3.13–18 is 3.1–4.12, which encompasses James' extended discussion of disorder and strife within the church. Apparently those who were causing the turmoil were claiming to have a superior wisdom, since James uses the words "wise" and "wisdom" four times in just six verses.

This is similar to Paul's treatise on wisdom in 1 Corinthians 1.17–2.5 where once again true wisdom is set over against disunity and disorder, just as it is in James. The trouble-makers James had in mind may have claimed to be wise, but James says if so, it's the wrong kind of wisdom. Its twin characteristics are "bitter jealousy" (literally, "harsh zeal," what J.H. Ropes describes as "the fierce desire to promote one's own opinion to the exclusion of those of others") and "selfish ambition" (the same word which Paul uses for "rivalry" in Phil 1.17), which are paired in verse 14 and again in 16. James locates this false wisdom in the "hearts" of those who are creating strife, a sign that he regards it as a serious spiritual disorder. The presence of such "wisdom" had led to boasting and falsehood. The presence of boasting is to be expected in such a context, but we can only wonder what sort of falsehoods it had produced.

"Wisdom"- But from Where?

James gets to the source of the problem in verse 15: "This is not the wisdom that comes down from above, but is earthly, unspiritual, demonic." Notice the contrast between heavenly ("from above") and "earthly." But James goes even further and characterizes this so-called wisdom as "unspiritual" and "demonic." It may masquerade as superior spiritual wisdom, but in reality it is inspired by demons. It's possible, of course, that James is using "demonic" in a figurative sense as a synonym for "evil," but it seems more likely that he means it literally. From what we read of them in the Gospels, the goal of the demons—those evil spirit beings who serve Satan—is to destroy the work of God, and according to 1 John 3.8, Jesus in turn came to "destroy the works of the devil." That's why we read of demons primarily in the Gospels, as they confronted Jesus (or were confronted by Him) during His earthly ministry. As He went about healing, they went about enslaving people and distorting the image of God within them. You only have to read Mark 5.1–20 to see the kind of chaos they brought into people's lives. These are the same evil beings who desire chaos within the body of Christ, only now they achieve it by inspiring a brand of "wisdom" that really isn't wise at all.

In verse 16 James cites the evidence that the wisdom claimed by the trouble-makers is not from heaven: it doesn't create peace. Rather, this sort of "wisdom" creates jealousy and selfish ambition, which leads to "disorder and every vile practice" (v 16). Any time a Diotrephes is present within a congregation, there will be chaos, and anyone who has ever dealt with a Diotrephes knows exactly what James is talking about. It is shocking the degree of confusion and sinful behavior that can arise within a church because of the presence of someone like Diotrephes, someone who operates by a "wisdom" that is purely self-centered and self-justifying.

James' contention that strife and chaos demonstrate lack of wisdom reflects the wisdom tradition of the Old Testament, as expressed in several texts from Proverbs:

Do not contend with a man for no reason, when he has done you no harm. (3.30)

A hot-tempered man stirs up strife, but he who is slow to anger quiets contention. (15.18)

A dishonest man spreads strife, and a whisperer separates close friends. (16.28)

The beginning of strife is like letting out water, so quit before the quarrel breaks out. (17.14)

Whoever meddles in a quarrel not his own is like one who takes a passing dog by the ears. (26.17)

As charcoal to hot embers and wood to fire, so is a quarrelsome man for kindling strife. (26.21)

No matter how wise a Diotrephes may claim to be, the strife he (or she) creates is evidence that if there is any wisdom present at all, it's the wrong kind from the wrong source.

The Real Deal

James isn't content simply to expose the source and character of false wisdom; he also explains its opposite, the "wisdom from above." Twice he describes heavenly wisdom by emphasizing that it comes "from above" (vv 15, 17). Remember that in 1.5 he said wisdom is God's gift; He alone is its true source. Such wisdom is first of all "pure" then "peaceable." Believers operating by the wisdom God supplies do not create strife and chaos. Rather, they will always be people who value peace. James goes on to say that such wisdom is also "gentle, open to reason, full of mercy and good fruits, impartial and sincere." Notice that each of these traits has to do with peace among believers and how we treat one another, and they are the very opposite of the demonic wisdom described in verses 15–16.

Above all, such wisdom promotes God's peace within the church. "Peace," in the biblical sense, is not merely the absence of strife, but *shalom* (the Hebrew word for "peace") in its fullest sense of well-being and wholeness. Wise Christians continually sow a "harvest of righteousness" in peace and are themselves peace-makers. Once again we hear the words of Jesus lying behind those of His brother: "Blessed are the peacemakers, for they shall be called sons of God" (Matt 5.9). A truly wise Christian—not one who merely *claims* to be wise—always seeks the peace of the church and wants the best for all of God's people. A Diotrephes, on the other hand, couldn't care less about the well-being of the church; he only cares about his own selfish ambition and agenda. So James' contrast is between the wisdom that leads to peace *versus* a so-called "wisdom" that leads to chaos and destruction. The difference is not subtle, but rather it is continually demonstrated in the behavior of those who create chaos as opposed to those who strive for peace.

Making—and Keeping—Peace Today

The challenge of distinguishing between true and false wisdom and maintaining peace within churches is as great today as it was when James wrote. We dare not be naive about the presence of such false wisdom in our midst and its potential to create exactly the kind of "disorder and every vile practice" James warns against. Here are some suggestions for coping with this challenge.

1. *Don't be surprised at the presence of "Diotrepheses" in the church.* Both James and 3 John serve as reminders that they have always been present and always will be. In Acts 20.28–31 Paul warned the elders of the church in Ephesus that "from among your own selves will arise men speaking twisted things, to draw away the disciples after them." Note the similarities with the false wisdom James describes. Such teachers operate from motives of "jealousy and selfish ambition" as they seek to gain a following for themselves. It doesn't matter what the "issue" is, and often such people will create one just to get attention. In 1 Timothy 1.3–7, a passage reminiscent of James 3.13–18, Paul speaks of "certain persons" who taught myths and speculations and genealogies because they were "desiring to be teachers of the law, without understanding either what they are saying or the things about which they make confident assertions." The specific issues may have been different from those in James, but the unhealthy desire to teach and the improper motives are clearly the same.

This doesn't mean we should become insensitive to the presence of the purveyors of false wisdom in our midst. Rather, it means we should not become discouraged when it happens or allow it to wreck our faith. It's simply one of the many spiritual pitfalls against which we need to be on guard ourselves.

2. *Those motivated by false wisdom should not be ignored or allowed to do their evil work.* Because such people *are* ambitious and self-assertive, we are often tempted to let them have their way or to try to ignore them. Yet when this happens, such people can gain a stranglehold on a church because no one exposes or confronts them. Scripture teaches that we are not to allow this to happen.

James certainly isn't content to sit by and let these people wreck the peace of the church(es) to whom he was writing. He seems to assume they were still present within the church, so he addresses the situation directly: "Do *you* want to be shown, *you foolish person*, that faith apart from works is useless?" (2.20). "Who is wise and understanding *among you*? By his good conduct let him show his works in the meekness of wisdom. But if *you* have bitter jealousy and selfish ambition…" (3.13–14). Likewise John doesn't merely complain about Diotrephes' bad behavior, but says, "if I come, I will bring up what he is doing, talking wicked nonsense against us" (3 John 10), clearly putting him on notice that he will not get away with his evil conduct. Paul tells the Ephesian elders to "take heed" and "be alert" to the presence of "wolves" in their midst so they can spot them and deal with them before they wreak havoc on the church. Later he instructs Titus to take note of contentious people and warn them not more than twice before avoiding them completely. Churches—and particularly church leaders—need to take these warnings seriously. The purveyors of false wisdom will arise again and again, and they must always be dealt with, or the church will pay a heavy price.

3. *Each of us must choose to live by the right kind of wisdom.* Every believer is faced with the choice of which of these two kinds of wisdom he will live by: the earthly, unspiritual, and demonic wisdom that leads to chaos and destruction, or the pure, peaceable,

heavenly wisdom that continually sows a harvest of righteousness. How can we be sure we are living by the right kind of wisdom?

First, continually check your own motives. Do you want what you want for the good of the church and to the glory of God or simply to satisfy your own selfish desires?

Second, deliberately pursue the kind of wisdom James promotes. No one is pure, peaceable, gentle, open to reason, etc. by accident, but only because we have set our hearts to become that way and because we are allowing God's Spirit to produce His fruit within us (Gal 5.22–23).

Third, always ask yourself if your attitudes and actions are promoting peace or stirring up strife. Constantly being embroiled in some sort of controversy or conflict is an indication that you are operating not by the wisdom from above but by that which is from below.

Back to James' question: "Who is wise and understanding among you?" Above all, make sure *you* are, in the truest, most spiritual sense.

How sweet, how heav'nly, is the sight, When those that love the Lord
In one another's peace delight, And so fulfill the Word.
When, free from envy, scorn and pride, Our wishes all above,
Each can his brother's failings hide, And show a brother's love.

Joseph Swain, "How Sweet, How Heavenly"

1/25/15

TWELVE | *The Three-Level War*

Some book titles are harder to forget than others. One that sticks with me is a title I came across years ago but can't forget, because the idea it expresses is so incongruous: *War in the Pews*. Another came along soon afterward that was on the same theme: *Worship Wars*. Both books decried the presence of strife in churches where the "Prince of Peace" is supposed to reign supreme and the tragedy that He so obviously doesn't due to the selfishness of those claiming to follow Him.

It would be nice to think that the language of warfare is an exaggeration, but then we come to James 4.1: "What causes quarrels and what causes fights among you? Is it not this, that your passions are at war within you?" James' word for "quarrels" is *polemai*, which literally means "wars." And his word for "fights" is *machai*, from the same root as the Greek word for "sword." Strife in the church is real, and it's sometimes nasty and bloody, and James forces us to take a long, hard look at why. It's important to know, not only so we can stop our pointless battles with one another but also so we can avoid them in the future.

An On-Going Conversation

James 4.1 isn't the first time James addresses the problem of strife in his letter. In fact, this discussion goes all the way back to 3.1, and 4.1–12 is actually the climax of what he began to say there. The scenario seems to be something like this. Since 3.1 addresses the problem of people teaching who shouldn't be, we can safely assume the core of the conflict lies there, with people who insisted they should be teachers but who weren't really qualified to do so. (See 1 Tim 1.3–7 for a similar problem addressed by Paul.) That's what leads to the discussion of the tongue, since the tongue is not only the teacher's primary tool but also the chief weapon in "church wars." James is emphatic that those who possess a true, godly wisdom will seek the peace of the church rather than fomenting chaos (3.17–18). Now in 4.1–12 he begins to deal with the underlying cause of the problem: "What causes quarrels and what causes fights among you?"

What James proposes is that these conflicts are actually wars taking place on three distinct but closely-related levels: the surface level (the "You Level"), the personal level (the "Me Level"), and the spiritual level (the "God Level").

Level One: "The Problem With Me Is You"

At the surface level, a conflict among brothers and sisters in Christ may appear to be rather cut-and-dried. For most of us, when we're part of such a conflict we see clearly what the problem is—the other person and his or her stubbornness, ignorance, lack of Christian spirit, etc. The disagreement may revolve around one or more "issues" between or among us, such as the manner of worship, use of church funds, a doctrinal disagreement, who is or who isn't in a leadership role, the correct translation of the Bible, or a host of other possibilities. (Sadly, we never seem to run short of such topics.)

Let me hasten to say that even within the church there are some battles worth fighting, as the Scriptures themselves make clear. Paul didn't hesitate to take a stand, even against a fellow apostle, where the basic truths of the gospel were in dispute, as in Galatians 2.11–12 and 6.13–17, or when his ministry was maligned by people who were envious of his role as an apostle, as in 2 Corinthians 11.12–14. Likewise, John wasn't about to stand by and let someone like Diotrephes take control of the church for his own purposes (3 John 9–10). The problem isn't the willingness to take a stand where truth and right are concerned but the wisdom to know which hills are worth dying on and which are not. Even more to the point, *it's being wise enough to see when the problem you think is the problem really isn't the problem at all.* In most church conflicts, the "presenting issue" turns out not to be the actual issue. People only *think* that's what the conflict is about, because it's easier to identify it that way and assume the high ground for themselves. But James won't let us get away with that. He presses us to go deeper.

Level Two: The Warfare Within

In 4.1b–2 James pulls the curtain of conflict aside to look backstage and see what's really going on when Christians fight. The real problem, he says, isn't the "issues" that we think are the problem; rather, it is "your passions…at war within you." The root cause of the warfare *without* is the warfare *within*. The word "passions" can also be translated "pleasures." It is our desire for self-gratification that is at war within us. We want what we don't have, so we "murder," and we covet and can't get what we want, so we "fight and quarrel." James' point is, when we are inwardly conflicted and frustrated, we tend to take it out on those around us. We're unhappy within ourselves, so we go at it with one another, and when that's the case almost any "issue" at hand will do as a pretense for the fight. The "issue" is merely a weapon; it isn't the cause of the conflict. That's why so many church fusses are so shockingly petty (color of the carpet, where to put the water fountain, the order of the worship service, etc.), because there are so many Christians just looking for a quarrel to pick due to their own unhappiness with themselves. It turns out that most church conflicts aren't about what the people involved think they're about.

But was James serious when he said "you *murder*"? Was he aware of people actually killing their brothers and sisters as a result of their conflicts? Here are some possible ways of understanding what he's getting at:

(1) Jewish literature frequently speaks of the abuse of the poor as "killing" them, as James says in 5.6: "You have condemned; you have murdered the righteous person. He does not resist you." We sometimes speak in the same exaggerated manner when we say to someone, "You're killing me!" when actually they're just taking advantage of us or causing pain in some way. Maybe James was saying, "When you get into these vicious conflicts in the church and are determined to have your own way, you end up abusing each other for your own ends." When that happens, we may not literally murder each other, but we do murder our unity and fellowship.

(2) On the other hand, James may have been speaking quite literally, only he is suggesting that even if no one has committed murder *yet*, the potential is there if the quarrels go unchecked. This would reflect the teaching of Jesus that to be angry with one's brother is closely akin to murder and that both make one liable to God's judgment (Matt 5.21–26). The act is simply the extension of the intent.

(3) A third possibility is that by "murder," James refers to verbal "killing," what we often call "character assassination." Has there ever been a church conflict in which this sort of behavior didn't take place? It seems impossible simply to disagree on an issue without attacking one another with our tongues and inflict-

ing some of the deepest wounds known to humanity, sometimes saying things that literally destroy another person's reputation or effectiveness in the kingdom.

Regardless of how we take James' "murder" language, one thing is clear: he takes the problem of quarrels within the church with deadly seriousness. And the root cause is not the other person but our own unsatisfied desires.

Level Three: Enmity With God

But James still hasn't gotten to the root of the problem, not until he begins to talk about the "God Level." In the latter part of verse 2 he says, "You do not have, because you do not ask." Part of the dissatisfaction described in verse 1 and the first part of verse 2 has to do with prayerlessness. Jesus said to "Ask and you will receive," so when we're lacking in what we desire it's often a sign of not asking for it. On the other hand, as James goes on to say in verse 3, sometimes even when we ask we don't receive, "because you ask wrongly, to spend it on your passions." (Here's that problem of selfishness again which James mentioned in verse 1.) In other words, even in our praying our motives are often impure, and we're asking, not for the glory of God's kingdom (which should always be the first concern of all our prayers—Matt 6.9–10), but for the fulfillment of our own selfish desires. Why? Simply because we are "adulterous people" who are at war with God. *Now* we arrive at the root of the problem: our unfaithfulness to our covenant relationship with God.

The language of adultery in verse 4 comes from the Old Testament prophets, who frequently portrayed Israel, the only nation with whom God had made a covenant, as an unfaithful wife betraying the goodness of her husband. This explains why James' word (translated in the ESV as "You adulterous people!") is actually feminine ("You adulteresses!"). The classic expression of this concept is the book of Hosea. The Lord tells the prophet to marry Gomer, a prostitute who, as their marriage progresses, demonstrates that in spite of Hosea's love and goodness, she will continue to pursue other lovers. Finally she is sold into slavery, but Hosea buys her back and again takes her as his wife. The entire sordid story is, of course, an acted parable of God's love for Israel and Israel's unfaithfulness in serving other gods. Likewise, in the first chapter of Isaiah the prophet levels the charge of adultery against Israel: "How the faithful city has become a harlot, she that was full of justice!" (Isa 1.21). In Jeremiah 3.6 God calls Israel "that faithless one," who "went up on every high hill and under every green tree, and there played the harlot." James now applies this concept to Christians who insist on "friendship with the world" rather than faithfulness to God, not recognizing that to befriend the world is to become God's enemy. To live in covenant relationship with God means to choose faithfulness to Him and to reject the ways of the unredeemed world. Not to make that choice, or to make it but go back on it, puts us at enmity with God.

In speaking as he does of "the world," it's obvious James doesn't mean "the created universe" or the people in it. After all, "God so loved the world that he gave his only Son…" Rather, James is speaking of "the world" in the same sense we most often find it in the Gospel of John and in the letter of 1 John, the world that is set in opposition to God and to His ways.

> Do not love the world or the things in the world. If anyone loves the world, the love of the Father is not in him. For all that is in the world—the desires of the flesh and the desires of the eyes and pride in possessions—is not from the Father but is from the world. And the world is passing away along with its desires, but whoever does the will of God abides forever. (1 John 2.15–17)

Scripture repeatedly challenges believers to declare and demonstrate loyalty to either God or the world. When we try to live between the two, there will be chaos in our lives spiritually, which will cause us to pray from selfish motives, which means we will not have what we desire, and we will be at odds with other believers whom we see as standing between us and what we want. It's not a pretty picture, but it's a realistic one and it explains "what causes quarrels" among the Lord's people.

In verse 5 James gives what looks like a quotation from Scripture, but which turns out not to be. The statement "He yearns jealously over the spirit that he has made to dwell in us" is found nowhere in the Bible, at least not in those exact words. It rather summarizes a general biblical theme of the holy jealousy of God for His covenant people, for the fact that He tolerates no rivals for our affection and service. One text which expresses this idea is Exodus 20.5: "…you shall not bow down to them or serve them; for I the Lord your God am a jealous God." Exodus 34.14 even goes so far as to say of God that "his name is Jealous." And Zechariah 8.2 says, "Thus says the Lord of hosts: I am jealous for Zion with great jealousy, and I am jealous for her with great wrath." To try to walk in the ways of the world sets us on a path at odds with our Creator and Lord. If we are to be His people, we must be His completely and not partially. (Remember the "double-minded man" of 1.6–8?) So James is saying something like "The Bible says that God is jealous for the affections of His people," but he isn't giving a direct quotation from Scripture.

In the context of James 3 and 4, the accusation of unfaithfulness leading to personal dissatisfaction leading to strife among brothers may refer primarily to people who had been seeking a leadership or teaching roles in the church simply so they could have their own way or so they could have the praise of others. On the other hand, the situation could be much more general and basic, referring simply to the fact that people were being selfish both in their praying and in their behavior toward one another. Either way, verses 1–5 provide a brilliant and penetrating analysis of the true source of human conflict among those who should be at peace.

What To Do?

Thankfully, as bad as this situation is, it's not hopeless, for in verse 6, just after declaring the holy jealousy of God, James says, "But he gives more grace." If not for this great truth, that God's grace outweighs His wrath, what hope would any of us have? Yet the decision to receive His grace remains with us, since James adds a quotation (or at least a paraphrase) from Proverbs 3.34, "God opposes the proud, but gives grace to the humble." If we humble ourselves before God, He is merciful and gracious; if we set ourselves in opposition to Him, we will find Him in opposition to us, a position no one should ever desire.

The remainder of this section of the letter, from verse 7 though verse 12, contains a series of nine imperatives ("submit," "resist," "draw near," "cleanse," "purify," "be wretched and mourn and weep," "let your laughter be turned to mourning and your joy to gloom," "humble yourselves," and "do not speak evil against one another"), all designed to correct the problems of fights and quarrels among believers and even more, to bring us in line with God's will so that the fighting will cease. We noted in our chapter on the author of James that one argument for identifying him as James the brother of Jesus is that he was obviously well known to his readers and was sufficiently respected to be able to command them and expect them to obey. This is nowhere more obvious than in verses 7–12.

Since God "opposes the proud, but gives grace to the humble," the most urgent response is to "Submit yourselves…to God."

Those in opposition to God must stop resisting His will and submit to His ways. Along with this, they must "resist the devil, and he will flee from you." This not only is an important command to stop playing into Satan's hands through our selfishness but also contains one of Scripture's most precious promises: standing up to Satan means he must flee. He has no choice. This isn't because of any power of our own, but because we have within us the Spirit of Him who was able to command even the unclean spirits, and they obeyed Him (Luke 4.36). So our victory is guaranteed; all we need do is resist. Paired with this great command coupled with a promise is another: "Draw near to God, and he will draw near to you." As surely as Satan will flee when we resist, God promises to draw near when we seek Him.

In response to double-mindedness, James says to cleanse both hands and hearts, that is to change behavior but also to be changed inwardly so that we are no longer motivated by selfishness. There needs to be a complete change of attitude, which is expressed in verse 9 by the imperatives to "be wretched and mourn and weep" and to exchange our frivolous spirit for one of mourning over our sinfulness and the inevitability of the judgment coming on those who continue to resist God. Verse 10 contains a third command coupled with a promise: "Humble yourselves before the Lord, and he will exalt you." Ironically, the way to exaltation is not through self-promotion but through humility, as James has previously suggested (1.9–10). Such a radical concept is in keeping with the teachings of Jesus regarding the standards in His kingdom: "But whoever would be great among you must be your servant, and whoever would be first among you must be your slave" (Matt 20.26–27). We should note that these words of our Lord were, like James' admonition, spoken to quarreling disciples.

James' final imperative in this section does not stand alone, but carries its own commentary with it: "Do not speak evil against one another, brothers" (v 11). The words which follow this admonition have a tightly-constructed logic: Speaking evil of (or slandering) a brother puts the slanderer in the role of judge; such an unqualified judge "judges the law," counting it as unworthy of being kept, because the law teaches against slander; being a judge of the law means one is not a doer of the law, and James has already established doing the law as a primary Christian responsibility (1.22); the only qualified lawgiver and judge is the one who can both save and destroy. So James ends with the logical question, "Who are you to judge your neighbor?" To do so makes one an impostor and a usurper, because he assumes a role that belongs to God alone. Slandering a brother or sister in Christ is far more serious an offense than we usually recognize.

The kind of warfare James describes in 4.1 should never go on in God's church. It doesn't have to occur, and it won't if we do as James advises. But we must have the wisdom to stop over-simplifying our conflicts with one another and to look within for the *real* source of our conflicts.

One heart, one Spirit, one voice to praise You.
We are the body of Christ.
One goal, one vision to see You exalted.
We are the body of Christ.
And to this we give our lives, to see You glorified.
One heart, one Spirit, one voice to praise You.
We are the body of Christ.

David B. Hampton and Scott Wesley Brown,
"We Are the Body of Christ"

*"For you are a mist that appears for a little time
and then vanishes."* (4.13–17)

THIRTEEN | *Business as Usual*

One of the qualities we Americans admire is self-determinism, the idea of making your own way, pulling yourself up by your bootstraps, and being self-made men and women. There never seems to be a shortage of success peddlers touting their sure-fire formulas for attaining wealth, if we're just willing to go for it (and pay for the materials they're selling). Every Spring at graduation time, speakers all over the land tell their youthful audiences, "You can be anything you want to be and do anything you want to do if you just want it badly enough." All of these folks tell us the only boundary to our success is ourselves, the sky is the limit, and if we dream big enough and plan big enough, we'll *be* big. "You can have it all" is the mantra of our materialistic society.

Naturally, there's some truth in the idea of self-determinism. How we do in life does depend to some extent on what kind of effort we do or don't put forth. But there are also some serious distortions of reality in this kind of thinking, and it is these distortions that James addresses in the last five verses of chapter four.

Who's in Control Here?

One reason James takes exception to the self-determination idea is that he was thoroughly steeped in the "Wisdom Tradition" of the Old Testament. This includes such books as Proverbs and Ecclesiastes, both of which punch sizeable holes in the human ego, especially when it comes to thinking we're completely in charge of what happens in the world or even in our own lives. James was undoubtedly familiar with such texts as Proverbs 16.9: "The heart of man plans his way, but the Lord establishes his steps." In other words, what happens in life is really *not* up to us and our plans and goals and dreams, at least not ultimately. Another wisdom text expressing a similar idea is Ecclesiastes 9.11–12: "Again I saw that under the sun the race is not to the swift, nor the battle to the strong, nor bread to the wise, nor riches to the intelligent, nor favor to those with knowledge, but time and chance happen to them all." Anyone who has closely observed life for any length of time knows this is true. Not everything is up to us, and much is totally beyond our control and not subject to our efforts.

Get Real!

And so James confronts those who don't seem to realize that life isn't all up to them. In verse 13 he begins his words of rebuke with "Come now" (as he does also in 5.1). This expression is a call to reality, something like "Surely you know better than that!" He addresses those who have their futures all planned out. "Today or tomorrow we will go into such and such a town and spend a year there and trade and make a profit." What we're reading about here is a business trip, and on the surface it sounds harmless enough. In fact, it's probably the way most people make their plans; they intend to do "business as usual."

But at another level this is an incredibly presumptuous statement. It assumes the planner knows (1) the time of the venture ("today or tomorrow"); (2) the place ("such and such a town"); (3) the length of stay ("a year"); (4) the activity ("trade"); and (5) even the outcome ("and get gain"). Given the uncertain circumstances of life (as Proverbs and Ecclesiastes express), no one should be so positive about what is going to happen. In verse 14 James points out two problems with making the kind of statement he quotes in verse 13.

First, we are far *too ignorant* of the future to speak so positively about it. "You do not know what tomorrow will bring," James says. To see the truthfulness of James' observation, think of your own life. Ten years ago, did you have any idea you would be living where you are today? Working at the job you now have? Not working at a job? Married to the person you're now married to? No longer married to the person you were once married to? Having the children or grandchildren you now have? Either enjoying the good health you now have or no longer having the health you once enjoyed? It doesn't take much reflection to see that James is right on target when he says "you *do not know* what tomorrow will bring."

The second problem with being over-confident about what the future holds is that we are *too temporary* to speak in this way. To drive home this point James first asks, "What is your life?," then answers his own question: "For you are a mist that appears for a little time and then vanishes." The point? You don't even know if you'll *be* here tomorrow, much less what you'll be doing if you are. Now this isn't the most uplifting thought in the Bible, but it's reality, and we all need to come to grips with it. Compared to the vast scope of eternity, our lives are a mere breath or vapor. The Bible is fond of using such ethereal imagery to describe the fragile nature of human existence. Job, facing the desperation of illness and overwhelming loss, asked God to "remember that my life is a breath" (Job 7.7). Psalms 39.4–6 offers this sober reminder:

> O Lord, make me know my end
> and what is the measure of my days;

let me know how fleeting I am!
Behold, you have made my days a few handbreadths,
    and my lifetime is as nothing before you.
Surely all mankind stands as a mere breath!
Surely a man goes about as a shadow!
Surely for nothing they are in turmoil;
    man heaps up wealth and does not
    know who will gather!

Psalms 78.39 declares that God is compassionate toward His wayward people because, "He remembered that they were but flesh, a wind that passes and comes not again." A case in point is the Rich Fool in Jesus' parable. After congratulating himself on his self-obtained security for a future of "many years," he was informed that "This night your soul is required of you" (Luke 12.16–20). All of this meshes with what James has already said in 1.9–11. The rich man passes away "like a flower of the grass" and "fades away in the midst of his pursuits."

Mist, breath, shadow, wind, withered grass—do you get the point? Life is an uncertain business, and we do well to remember that. We will all leave this life with unfinished plans and projects, unachieved goals, unwritten books, unmended relationships, unmade trips and unmade beds, things we thought we would accomplish but simply ran out of days for doing them. So to make the kind of concrete (James would say boastful—v 16) plans that James describes is really pretty foolish.

So, No Plans?

I can imagine at about this point you might be thinking, "Wait a minute! Does this mean it's wrong to make plans—ever, about anything?" Should the temporal and uncertain nature of life make us shrink back from the future and just live in anticipation of death, looking forward to nothing, planning nothing, and risking nothing? Is James suggesting a fatalistic approach to life?

In a word, no. The Bible doesn't condemn plan-making, just the practice of making plans as though their accomplishment lies solely with us. After all, we read several times of Paul making plans for his various evangelistic forays around the Mediterranean, and I suspect he knew the same texts James had in his own background. For example, toward the end of his great letter to the Romans (15.22–29), he states his intention to travel to Spain for further evangelistic work and to stop by to see the Romans (and get some support from them) on his way. And before that he intended to travel to Jerusalem to deliver financial help for the poor in that city. Likewise, in Acts 15.36 we learn that what we call the "Second Missionary Journey" had a rather specific purpose and plan behind it: "Let us return and visit the brothers in every city where we proclaimed the word of the Lord, and see how they are." Paul knew where he planned to go, whom he planned to visit, and what he intended to do when he got there. It's difficult to conclude that there is anything inherently wrong with plan-making. (Although note that in the last example, Paul's plans were changed by the Holy Spirit.)

So what is the error James is criticizing? Simply put, it's the tendency to make plans without factoring in the will of God. Regardless of our plans—whether they concern business, family, church, retirement, or whatever—they are all to be submitted to God's will. "Instead you ought to say, 'If the Lord wills, we will live and do this or that.'" The point isn't so much the repetition of the words, as if that somehow sanctifies our activities, but rather the attitude of recognition that what we think is going to happen and what God knows will happen or desires to happen may not be the same thing. The mere recitation of the formula "if the Lord wills" could become a meaningless formula thoughtlessly uttered, but not if we cultivate the attitude that all of our plans are subject to God's overruling.

Paul again supplies a helpful example. When he paid a brief first visit to Ephesus, he preached in the local synagogue. The people there asked him to stay for a longer period than he had intended but he declined, and when he left them he said, "I will return to you if God wills" (Acts 18.19–21). As it turned out, God did will for Paul to return, because Acts 19.1 says on the Third Missionary Journey, "Paul passed through the inland country and came to Ephesus," where he remained for a total of three years (19.10, 20.31). Also, in Romans 1.10 Paul expressed his long-held desire to visit the Roman church, "asking that somehow by God's will I may now at last succeed in coming to you." And, as we saw in Romans 15.22–29, he had a specific plan for doing so. Making such plans according to the Lord's will seems to have been a definite pattern with Paul, since he also told the Corinthians, "But I will come to you soon, if the Lord wills… " (1 Cor 4.19). Notice that Paul doesn't say he knows what God's will is or will be. None of us is guaranteed a blueprint of what lies ahead of us. Rather, he simply leaves his plans open to the reality that God may have other ideas that Paul as yet knew nothing about.

Plans aren't the problem; rather, the problem is the failure to take God into account as we make our plans. James calls this "arrogant boasting" and "evil" in verse 16. The word "arrogance" is from a Greek word (*alazoneia*) which describes the person who has an unrealistic view of his or her own status and power. The ancient Greeks used this word to describe orators, philosophers, quack physicians, and government officials who promise more than they could deliver. James says, to plan your life without including or consulting God—in other words, to carry on "business as usual"—is simply evil. Why "evil"? Because it's actually a form of idolatry, in which we elevate ourselves and our wills and our plans above anything God might have in mind for us. That has to be evil.

Yet how many Christians do exactly what James condemns? How many choose a career, decide where to live, start a business, or decide whom to marry without even considering that God should be taken into account? If it's wrong to plan a simple business trip in that spirit, as James says it is, then surely it's wrong to make larger decisions without considering what God might have to say about it.

Do the Right Thing!

Almost as though he's afraid someone might miss his point, James states it emphatically again in the final verse of chapter 4: "So whoever knows the right thing to do and fails to do it, for him it is sin" (v 17). We often hear this verse applied in a general way to the effect that it's always sinful to know what's right and not do it, leading to what used to be called "sins of omission," when we know what we should have done but didn't do it. Perhaps the verse has some validity in a general context (but we need to be careful with it—after all, who always does *everything* he knows is right?), but in the context of this paragraph its application is quite specific. Here it means that the failure to include God in our plans, to go about business as usual, isn't just foolish or bad, it's a *sin*. It's an exercise in what some describe as "practical atheism"— not denying that God exists but living as though He doesn't.

So, James says, do the right thing: acknowledge God in all you do. Include Him in every plan. Recognize His power over every moment of your incredibly brief life. "Come now!" Give up thinking you're in charge.

I don't know about tomorrow, I just live from day to day;
I don't borrow from its sunshine, For its skies may turn to gray;

I don't worry o'er the future, For I know what Jesus said,
And today I'll walk beside Him, For He knows what is ahead.
Many things about tomorrow I don't seem to understand;
But I know who holds tomorrow, And I know who holds my hand.

Ira Stanphill, "I Know Who Holds Tomorrow"

"Your gold and silver have corroded, and their corrosion will be evidence against you and will eat your flesh like fire." (5.1–6)

FOURTEEN | *The Rust of Riches*

Have you ever heard of the "Roby Millionaires"? How about the "Roby 43"? Roby, Texas is a farming community of just a few hundred people located not far from where I grew up, so I was intrigued to hear in 1997 that 43 residents of that little community had become instant millionaires by pooling their money together and winning the Texas Lottery. Their story went world-wide almost overnight, with the town being covered in the national media and various members of the "43" appearing on the talk show circuit. Roby is a hard-luck town where most folks barely get by, but with that windfall it gained the distinction of being the town with the highest per capita number of millionaires in the entire United States.

But that's not the whole story. In a follow-up television program several years later, I learned that most of the instantaneous millionaires had gone broke, that there were deep divisions within the community and especially among the "43" themselves—and even within their families—over their new-found wealth. Some of the "lucky 43" had died tragically. Even all those millions of dollars didn't make the town a happier, more prosperous place, and today it still struggles to survive, a sadder—and hopefully a wiser—place. Money wasn't the answer. It seldom is.

"Come Now!"

Even though most of us think getting rich is one of the best things that could ever happen, what James has to say to and about the rich isn't flattering or encouraging and should make you think twice before deciding to join their ranks. Remember that in 1.10 James says the rich brother should boast "in his humiliation, because like the flower of the grass he will pass away." In 2.1–5 he chastises his readers for showing favoritism to the rich visitors who came to their worship assemblies, because these were the very people who were oppressing the believers and were "the ones who blaspheme the honorable name by which you were called." His illustration of "faith without works" in 2.14–17 involves someone who has sufficient assets to assist the poor with food and clothing but instead of helping, simply says, "Go in peace, be warmed and filled." In 4.1–3 he condemns covetousness (literally "the desire for more") and friendship with the world and pinpoints selfish desires as the reason for strife within the Christian community. And, just before the text we're now examining, he rebukes the merchants, who obviously weren't poor, for planning their business without considering God's will in the matter. But he has saved his harshest words to the rich for near the end of the letter, where for the second time he says, "Come now," this time addressed to "you rich" who need to "weep and howl for the miseries that are coming upon you." The "Come now" echoes his words to the business person who made plans without God in them (4.13), as he continues to chastise those who have placed materials things first in their lives and affections.

In order to understand what's going on in this part of the letter, we need to ask, "Who were these people?" The evidence suggests they were not rich people within the church(es) to whom James wrote but the non-Christian rich among whom they lived. Most commentators think they were likely the wealthy land owners who habitually oppressed the poor in order to keep them poor and to keep themselves wealthy. Here's why they think so.

First, there is a sharp contrast between James' words to "you rich" in 5.1 and his more consoling words in 5.7: "Be patient, therefore, *brothers*, until the coming of the Lord." The "brothers" here does not seem to be accidental or incidental, but rather indicates a shift in the intended audience. He's been denouncing the sinful rich. Now he offers encouragement to the long-suffering "brothers."

Second, remember that 2.7 has already suggested that "the rich" are not among the believers, since James asks, "Are not the rich the ones who oppress you, and the ones who drag you into court?" Again, there is a clear contrast between the oppressed "you" (believers) and "the rich."

Third, notice that James holds out no hope at all to "the rich" he addresses in 5.1–6. He simply admonishes them to "weep and howl" because of the coming judgment and doesn't even call for their repentance. This would not likely be the case if he thought of "the rich" as brothers who needed to mend their ways in order to avoid judgment.

So why would he address the non-Christian rich in a letter to Christians? What would be the point unless they were part of the intended audience of the letter and could benefit from James' "Come now" admonition? The answer lies in James' close affinity with the Old Testament prophets, who frequently addressed their prophetic oracles (messages) to audiences who would never hear them, such as the nations who oppressed Israel and were destined to experience God's wrath because of it. Joel 3.4–8 provides a typical example:

> What are you to me, O Tyre and Sidon, and all the regions of Philistia? Are you paying me back for something? If you are

paying me back, I will return your payment on your own head swiftly and speedily. For you have taken my silver and my gold, and have carried my rich treasures into your temples. You have sold the people of Judah and Jerusalem to the Greeks in order to remove them far from their own border. Behold, I will stir them up from the place to which you have sold them, and I will return your payment on your own head. I will sell your sons and your daughters into the hand of the people of Judah, and they will sell them to the Sabeans, to a nation far away, for the Lord has spoken.

Obviously Joel didn't expect the people of Tyre and Sidon and the Philistines to hear or read his oracle. His words were for the comfort and encouragement of Israel, but they are spoken as if the nations were in fact present to hear them. This is apparently what happens in James 5.1–6 as well, as James issues what Peter Davids, in his commentary on James, describes as "a sharp, cutting cry of prophetic denouncement" (*The Epistle of James: A Commentary on the Greek Text*, 175). The goal isn't the repentance of the rich but the comfort of oppressed believers by telling them what will eventually happen to their oppressors.

Four Deadly Sins

Once James has spoken his "Come now" to the rich, he begins to enumerate their sins. The exposure of these sins is not something unique to James or even something uniquely Christian. The Law of Moses had, centuries before, spoken eloquently against the practices James describes, and they are likewise reflected in the teachings of Jesus as well.

1. Hoarding. Verses 2–3 declare the deteriorated condition of wealth unused and unshared. "Your riches have rotted and your garments are moth-eaten." Keeping in mind that money was not so much the common medium of exchange in ancient societies as it is today, the "riches" probably indicate grain which has been stored until it has rotted. It's hard for an experienced Bible reader not to hear in these words echoes of Jesus' "Parable of the Rich Fool," the story of the man who, confronted with a bumper grain crop, chose to tear down his barns and build bigger ones rather than share his excess with those in need (Luke 12.13–21). It was a defiant act of refusal to use his excess to bless those who had little or nothing. The rich man in the parable, like "the rich" in James, "laid up treasure for himself" and was not "rich toward God" due to this refusal to share.

"Garments" were also a common medium of exchange and an indication of wealth in the ancient Middle East, as reflected in numerous Old Testament texts. Genesis 45.21–22 says that after Joseph revealed himself to his brothers, he gave each of them "a change of clothes, but to Benjamin he gave three hundred shekels of silver and five changes of clothes." At the outset of Israel's conquest of their Promised Land, Achan sinned when he took, along with a quantity of silver and gold, "a beautiful cloak from Shinar" (Josh 7.21). Samson's wager with his wedding guests was that, if they could solve his riddle, he would give them "thirty linen garments and thirty changes of clothes," and they would do likewise if they couldn't solve it (Jdg 14.12–13). Part of the honorific gift which Naaman took to the king of Israel to secure his help for Naaman's healing was "ten changes of clothes" (2 Kgs 5.5). That clothing continued to be considered an indication of wealth is reflected in Paul's declaration in Acts 20.33 that, while living among the Ephesians, "I coveted no one's silver or gold or apparel." Jesus' words in Matthew 6.19–20 indicate the same: "Do not lay up for yourselves treasures on earth, where moth and rust destroy and where thieves break in and steal, but lay up for yourselves treasures in heaven, where neither moth nor rust destroys and where thieves do not break in and steal." The reference to "moths" shows that Jesus had in mind stored garments as part of one's stockpile of "treasures."

Verse 3 scolds the rich for the fact that "your gold and silver have corroded." Technically, gold and silver don't "rust," but they can accumulate a kind of surface corrosion and discoloration. The point here isn't that the riches have actually deteriorated and so have been wasted but that they remain *unused*. They have not been put in the service of either God or man, and their corrosion will serve as "evidence against you and will eat your flesh like fire." In other words, at judgment, the evidence of wealth unused but merely kept for the sake of having it will argue powerfully for the condemnation of the rich, because it will testify that their priorities and affections in life were seriously skewed. They will testify that, although wealthy in material things, the rich were spiritually bankrupt because in Jesus' words, they were not "rich toward God."

2. Withholding wages from the poor. The Old Testament could not be more explicit concerning what God thinks of this sin:

> You shall not oppress a hired servant who is poor and needy, whether he is one of your brothers or one of the sojourners who are in your land within your towns. You shall give him his wages on the same day, before the sun sets (for he is poor and counts on it), lest he cry against you to the Lord, and you be guilty of sin. (Deut 4.14–15)

> You shall not oppress your neighbor or rob him. The wages of a hired servant shall not remain with you all night until the morning. (Lev 19.13)

Notice that in these two texts withholding wages from a poor person is the same as robbery, and the one who withholds is in danger of the outcry of the oppressed, which the Lord will surely hear. James must have had these and other similar texts in mind when he wrote in verse 4, "Behold, the wages of the laborers who mowed your fields, which you kept back by fraud, are crying out against you, and the cries of the harvesters have reached the ears of the Lord of hosts." The reference to God as "the Lord of hosts" is an expression found frequently in the Prophets and contains an implied threat. It's a title which describes God at the head of His armies, poised to avenge His people. No one would want to be found in the position James describes, but the rich, by violating God's law so blatantly, have placed themselves squarely in His sights for judgment.

3. An extravagant life-style. The first half of verse 5 identifies this sin: "You have lived on the earth in luxury and in self-indulgence." While others were in need, these people enjoyed abundance and didn't share it. James' words remind us of Jesus' story of the Rich Man and Lazarus (Luke 16.19–31). Jesus offers no criticism of the rich man, only describing him as wearing nice clothing and eating good food. His sin lay in the fact that the beggar at his gate went without while he had more than enough.

No doubt the rich James describes saw themselves as doing nothing wrong. After all, in their minds at least, their wealth was the result of their shrewdness and hard work and was theirs to dispose of as they pleased. James sees it differently. In the second half of verse 5 he describes them as having "fattened their hearts for a day of slaughter." In the Old Testament a "fat heart" was a sign of ignoring God and refusing to hear and obey His word (Isa 6.10, Psa 119.70). The rich James addresses were really fattening their hearts in preparation to be slaughtered. They were like cattle gorging themselves on all that was available to them, not realizing that their fattening would only hasten their deaths.

4. Oppression of the righteous. James' accusation in verse 6 is quite graphic: "You have condemned; you have murdered the righteous person. He does not resist you." As mentioned in Chapter Two, "the poor" and "the righteous" are often equated in Jewish literature, and they seem to be so in James. Previously in this paragraph James spoke of the poor laborers whose wages had been kept back from them, but now he speaks of "the righteous person," and the two likely reference the same group—the dispossessed to whom James was originally written.

Had some of them actually been "murdered"? It's certainly not impossible, especially once we recognize that the rich were not the Christian rich. It was not unknown in Jewish history for a rich person to kill a poorer one in order to take possession of his property. This is exactly what Ahab and Jezebel did to Naboth in order to get his vineyard (1 Kgs 21.1–16). On the other hand, we have already seen in our discussion of 4.2 that "murder" can be used in a figurative sense of seriously depriving someone or of "killing" them by slander. In the setting James describes, any of these seems to be a lively possibility. At the very least, the poor (i.e., righteous) had been seriously abused. Some of the rich may have literally starved to death the poor laborers who worked in their fields by refusing to pay them.

So ends James' indictment of the rich. Their sins were many, brutal, and heartless, and they could expect nothing other than God's judgment in return. Not a very wise way to live.

"Is It I, Lord?"

I don't know about you, but I find this a disturbing passage of Scripture. Why? Because by any realistic definition of "rich," I am one. Especially if we take seriously Paul's definition in 1 Timothy 6.8–9. Paul says "if we have food and clothing, with these we will be content. But those who desire to be rich..." Did you catch that? Being rich, by Paul's standards, is to have more than food and clothing. And he says it's dangerous to want more, but most of us do, don't we?

Is this just Paul? I hardly think so. Remember that Jesus' description of the rich man in the parable of the Rich Man and Lazarus was simply that he ate well and dressed well. Which of us does that not describe? Sure, we may not have as much as some folks we know, but if we eat well, dress well, have a place to live, get decent medical care, and have something to drive, we're light-years ahead of most of the world. Let's face it: We're rich.

Even if James' words aren't addressed to the *Christian* rich, I don't feel much better about them, because all of the sins he lists in verses 1–6 can be committed by a believer. In fact, the Bible contains many warnings against the abuse of wealth, and almost all of them are directed to God's people. Remember, it was to Israel that Malachi addressed the penetrating question, "Will a man rob God?" (Mal 3.6–12), and Jesus told the parables of the Rich Fool and the Rich Man and Lazarus to His followers, not to outsiders. The abuse of wealth is a serious sin, and Christians are just as prone to it as anyone else.

Think of the sins of hoarding and extravagance, for example. Because we live in a society that encourages both, applauds those who hoard the most, and admires those who live the most extravagantly, these two sins are actually *goals* for many believers. And both statistics and experience prove that the more one has, the less likely one is willing to give to help others or to promote the cause of God. So I'm concerned lest I and others around me become blinded to the truth of what James is saying. For example, when does saving and investing for the future become hoarding? The boundary isn't always obvious, is it? At what point does a little better life-style become extravagance in God's sight? Oh, it's easy to point a finger at the super-rich and decry *their* excesses, but what about the more modest ones of my own? And how well do I have a right to live and how much do I have a right to keep for myself when others are in need, especially when that need is for the gospel of Christ? At what point do I become the rich man feasting on the riches of God's kingdom while a dying world lies at my doorstep? Do I have a "right" to treat myself to luxuries simply because I can, realizing that others lack the basic necessities of life, even of eternal life?

It occurs to me that, while society encourages me to get and keep all I can and live as well (materially) as I can, Jesus never once criticized anyone for not making enough money or warned anyone against not having a large enough savings portfolio or urged anyone to seek a higher standard of living. In fact, His words were always in the other direction, just as James' words are. "Take care, and be on your guard against all covetousness, for one's life does not consist in the abundance of his possessions" (Luke 12.15). "How difficult it will be for those who have wealth to enter the kingdom of God!" (Mark 10.23).

And we hear the voice of James saying, "Amen! Come now, you rich...."

Jesus calls us; o'er the tumult Of our life's wild restless sea,
Day by day His sweet voice soundeth, Saying "Christian, follow me."
Jesus calls us from the worship Of the vain world's golden store;
From each idol that would keep us, Saying, "Christian, love me more."

Cecil F. Alexander, "Jesus Calls Us"

"Be patient therefore, brothers, until the coming of the Lord." (5.7–12)

FIFTEEN | *Hang in There!*

Remember not many years ago when Internet service was so much slower than it is now? Yet no matter how much it has improved, somehow it's never fast enough. We stand in fast food lines, but no matter how good the service, we never seem to get our food quickly enough. And how annoying is it when there's someone ahead of you in traffic who's going just a bit slower than you want to go? No wonder someone has dubbed 21st-Century American society as "The Can't Wait Society"! So many things get our blood pressure up, because we don't think we should have to wait for anything.

This problem is so widespread that we make jokes about it: "Lord, give me patience—and do it now!" But it's actually a very serious matter, one that James addresses in this very practical letter. What could be more practical than our need for patience, and what could be wiser than to seek it?

Patience in Tough Times

Why does James speak of patience at this point in his letter? Is it simply because this is a common human problem, or is there something more specific going on in the lives of his first readers? The first six verses of James 5 suggest that the latter is the case. James has just finished chastising the rich for hoarding their goods, withholding wages from their poor laborers, and taking advantage of the poor in other ways as well. Now in verse 7 he says, "Be patient, *therefore*, brothers..." The "therefore" shows that what he says in verses 7–12 is based on what he has just finished saying. This suggests that the patience James calls for is needed because of the abuses being heaped on his dispossessed readers. Note also that whereas James spoke to "you rich" in 5.1, he now speaks to his "brothers," a term he uses four times in these six verses. They need patience, because the circumstances they're dealing with are tough and aren't likely to change any time soon.

A Hazard to Spiritual Health

Before analyzing verses 7–12, we should notice why James is so concerned about the potential lack of patience. Impatience places us in spiritual danger on several fronts.

Impatience often causes us to mistreat other people. Just because we are being mistreated (or think we are), we have no excuse for being short-tempered or unkind to those around us. Paul said "Love is patient and kind" (1 Cor 13.4), which means it's impossible to be both loving and impatient. We see evidence of this every day, as impatience adds to the already-chronic erosion of good manners in our society. Someone slows us down in traffic, so we honk just to let them we know we caught them doing something we consider inexcusable. There is far less respect for the elderly than in former times, mostly because they're so slow-moving and tend to get in our way. In Titus 3.2 Paul says we are to "show perfect courtesy to all people." That won't happen if we allow our impatience to go unchecked.

Impatience often disrupts Christian fellowship, and this is probably much closer to James' concern than simply everyday impatience with those we encounter. In 5.9 he urges us not to grumble (or "stop grumbling") against one another. There's something of a logical disconnect at work when this happens. Others mistreat us, but we take it out on those closest to us who perhaps have nothing to do with the mistreatment. And even if they do in some way irritate us, we still are not at liberty to grumble against them. It's hard to experience unity with people when you're constantly complaining about them.

Impatience can cause us to sin. First Samuel 13 provides a memorable example of this negative impact of impatience. King Saul was about to go into battle against the dreaded Philistines, but he needed to wait for the prophet Samuel to come and offer the necessary sacrifices. He waited the seven days that Samuel had told him to wait, but Samuel didn't come, and the people, who were unsure of the outcome of this battle anyway, began to scatter. So Saul decided to offer the sacrifices himself, which was an intrusion into Samuel's role as priest and something Saul had no right to do. No sooner had he completed the sacrifice than Samuel arrived, demanding to know what Saul had done. Saul tried to make excuses (even claiming he had to "force himself" to do it), but Samuel declared that his act was foolish and in violation of God's command. And all because he couldn't wait another minute to do the right thing. As a result, this violation of God's boundaries was a factor in Saul's eventually losing his throne and his life. James has this same concern for his readers: he doesn't want them to "be judged" (i.e., "condemned") and "fall under condemnation" (5.9, 12).

Patience Isn't a "Suggestion"

Given the dangers of impatience, it's not at all surprising that James commands his readers to "be patient." In fact, there are seven imperatives in these six verses: "Be patient." "You also, be patient." "Establish your hearts." "As an example of suffering and

PROMISE?
vow? pledge? MATT 5:33
take an oath?
Hang in There! | 139

patience, brothers, take the prophets." "Do not swear." "Let your 'yes' be yes and your 'no' be no." It's hard to miss James' point: Being patient and impatient are *choices* we make, not natural endowments of temperament. It may be more difficult for some to practice patience than for others, but it's still possible, and James places us all under the obligation to do it.

James isn't alone in that, because we find the same emphasis in Paul's writings. "Put on then, as God's chosen ones, holy and beloved, compassion, kindness, humility, meekness, and patience, bearing with one another and, if one has a complaint against another, forgiving each other; as the Lord has forgiven you, so you also must forgive" (Col 3.12–13). "But the fruit of the Spirit is love, joy, peace, patience, kindness, goodness, faithfulness, gentleness, self-control" (Gal 5.22–23). "I charge you in the presence of God and of Christ Jesus, who is to judge the living and the dead, and by his appearing and his kingdom: preach the word; be ready in season and out of season; reprove, rebuke, and exhort, with complete patience and teaching" (2 Tim 4.1–2).

Here's the bottom line: We have no entitlement to impatience. We usually think we have good reasons for becoming so impatient. But Scripture says there isn't a single one; rather, by impatience we place ourselves in danger of God's judgment.

Here's What I Mean...

Now that James has given us a grasp of the significance of patience for Christian living, we need to ask, just what does he mean by "patience"? If we think of the person who passively endures whatever comes without any complaint or effort to change the situation, we'll miss the point. I'm reminded of a news report that featured a Central American woman who lived on the slopes of an erupting volcano. When asked if she intended to flee she replied, "No, I'll just be patient and see what happens." That's fatalism, not "patience" in the biblical sense, certainly not in James' meaning of it. Let's notice first of all the terminology he uses to express it.

James uses two different Greek words which have very similar meanings. It's unlikely he intends to draw any sharp distinctions between them by using both, but he does so in order to express shades of meaning and possibly for the sake of variety. The word *makrothymia* and its related verb (vv 7 [twice], 8, 10) literally mean "long-tempered" and suggest being slow to anger. *Hypomone* (twice in v 11) implies courageous resistance, endurance, and fortitude in the face of hardship. Notice that neither suggests passive resignation to things as they are but rather the willingness to endure until better things come. The waiting period may be one of intense activity, as we'll see below, but even if it isn't, it will surely be a time of active prayer and faith, not resignation.

Perhaps even more helpful than the words James uses for "patience" are the examples he offers.

The Farmer (v 7). This example reminds us that some things simply can't be rushed. Granted, the period of waiting for the fruits of his labor may involve doing other things in the meantime, but much of the task of farming is beyond the farmer's control. There's nothing to do but wait for the rain and for the eventual growth of the seed. Such an attitude of patience requires trust in God's timing and in the certainty that what God has promised will come to pass. The "early" rains are those needed to cause the seed to germinate, while the "late" ones propel the crop to maturity and the eventual harvest. Both are out of the control of the farmer and are in the hands of God.

So what does this suggest we should do when we have waited and waited but still haven't seen the desired results in our lives, in spite of all our "sowing and watering" and even our praying? It's simple: we wait and refuse to give up as we trust that God will eventually keep all of His promises. Isn't this what Paul is getting at in Galatians 6.9 when he says, "And let us not grow weary of doing good, for in due season we will reap *if we do not give up*"? If things aren't happening in your life as you want them or when you want them, wait. "You also be patient" (v 8), James says, and "Establish your hearts" (v 9), which is another way of saying, "Be patient." The verb for "establish" suggests a steadfast resolve, a determination not to be thrown off course in spite of all obstacles. Our greatest need when facing distress may be simply to accept God's timing, believing He will act when He knows it is best.

The Prophets (vv 10-11a). "Suffering and patience," the virtues exemplified by the Old Testament prophets, is likely a way of saying, "suffering *in* (or *with*) patience." We need only to remember the ministries of men such as Elijah, Jeremiah, Ezekiel, Daniel, and others to get James' point. The prophets all brought messages to Israel and Judah which were far from popular, and they suffered tremendously as a result. Yet they had no choice but to proclaim the message God had given them, to "speak in the name of the Lord" as James says, and to take their sufferings patiently.

Yet who would question the value of what they did or their special role in proclaiming the will of God? Likewise, there will be some things in your life that you know from Scripture are right and good but from which you don't see immediate positive results. There may even be prolonged periods of waiting and/or suffering, just as there was with the prophets, because you are doing the right thing. But as James says, "Behold, we consider those blessed who remained steadfast" (v 11a). There is a special form of blessing for those who consistently, doggedly do what they know to be right, as James' next example demonstrates.

Job (v 11b). While "the patience of Job" has become a proverbial way of describing those who accept their suffering in silence, that's hardly what the Book of Job says about its main (after God, that is) character. Unfortunately, most folks' knowledge of Job doesn't extend past the first two chapters, where Job loses everything yet continues to say things such as, "The Lord gave, and the Lord has taken away; blessed be the name of the Lord," and the narrator can still say, "In all this Job did not sin or charge God with wrong" (1.21–22). Likewise, at the end of the book Job receives double all that he had in the beginning (except for his children), so that the story, if we read only chapters 1–2 and the last chapter, has a kind of fairy-tale, happily-ever-after quality about it. But have you ever read chapters 3–41? If so, you know that Job's relationship with the Lord became stormy and he *did* charge Him with wrong, so that before the book ends he must "repent in dust and ashes" (42.6). Job's story is far more true-to-life than a cursory reading of the first two and the last chapters would lead us to believe. At various points in the book, such as in chapter 7, Job begs God simply to leave him alone and let him die and announces, "Therefore I will not restrain my mouth; I will speak in the anguish of my spirit; I will complain in the bitterness of my soul" (7.11). That isn't exactly what we mean when we speak of some dear suffering saint as having "the patience of Job," is it?

So in what sense *was* Job "patient"? It's probably not by accident that James uses the particular word for "steadfastness" to describe Job. His "patience"/steadfastness lay in the fact that he never gave up. In spite of his accusations against God, he refused to turn away from Him or even to deny his own integrity as his friends urged him to do. And although he had absolutely no understanding of what was happening to him or why, Job toughed it out with God and found the Lord to be "compassionate and merciful" in spite of all he had to endure. And we should not fail to note the book ends without Job *ever* having any understanding of why all this had happened to him.

What did this mean for James' first readers, the dispossessed of the First Century who were suffering abuse and oppression at the hands of the unrighteous rich and who understood the meaning of injustice far more clearly than most of us could ever imagine? Just this: they were never to give up trusting God, believing that in His own good time He would right all wrongs. And for us? It's still the same: "Be patient, therefore, brothers."

The End Is in Sight!

Merely telling us to "be patient" without letting us in on the end game might seem heartless and empty. But that isn't what James does. There is a decisive end-point for all oppression and unrighteousness, and none of his readers—either then or now—should lose sight of that victory for a moment. Suffering and injustice are not infinite, nor do they have the last word in God's universe.

So James doesn't say simply, "Be patient," but "Be patient *until the coming of the Lord*" (v 7). And when he urges us to "establish our hearts," he again points toward the great motivation that "the coming of the Lord is at hand" (v 8). The return of Christ and the final judgment are not simply about punishing wrong-doers, but they also signal the ultimate reign of God over all creation, so that God's will is truly done "on earth as it is in heaven." It is a time when all wrongs will be righted, when all wrong-doing will, indeed, be punished, but when also those who have suffered patiently receive the reward God longs to give them.

What does "at hand" mean in this context? Probably nothing more than that the Lord could come at any time, so we must always be ready for Him. Jesus Himself had taught the same, so it isn't hard to imagine where James had learned this great truth (see Matt 24.36, 42, 44). We should live every day in light of eternity, in anticipation of seeing the Savior face to face, and of receiving the blessings He has promised. It's the only wise way to live.

There is still a third reference to Jesus' return in these verses, however. As James warns against grumbling against one another, he says not to do so, "so that you may not be judged," then reminds us that "the Judge is standing at the door" (v 9). Again we are reminded of the immediacy of Christ's coming, as well as of His unseen presence. He is "at the door" hearing every conversation, and He stands ready to re-enter the scene of human history to bring it to its grand finale. We can never allow ourselves to forget that. We must never fail to be patient and steadfast no matter what we're going through or long we have to go through it.

In short, continue to trust God always. Treat one another well even when there seems to be every justification for doing otherwise. And never let your circumstances, no matter how bad, cause you to forget the coming of the Lord.

> *And, Lord, haste the day when the faith shall be sight,*
> *The clouds be rolled back as a scroll,*
> *The trump shall resound and the Lord shall descend,*
> *"Even so" it is well with my soul.*

Horatio G. Spafford, "It Is Well With My Soul"

"...let your 'yes' be yes and your 'no' be no, so that you may not fall under condemnation." (5.12)

SIXTEEN | *The Simple Truth*

So far in our study of James, we've been looking at whole paragraphs, sometimes more, but at this point we'll focus on only one verse, the one about telling the simple truth. Why just this one verse? Well, for one thing James says it's important: "But *above all*, my brothers..." In giving his instructions for wise living to dispossessed believers, for some reason he singles out this particular bit of wisdom as particularly significant. In fact, it's so important that ignoring it could lead to our condemnation, according to the last clause of verse 12.

That's reason enough, but there's more. Read verse 12 in the ESV or any other fairly recent translation, and you'll notice it stands alone as an independent paragraph. Of course, it's not that way in the Greek manuscripts (which aren't paragraphed), but this is what translators have done with it. Or, you might say, it's what they haven't done with it, because making it its own paragraph is a way of not making a decision about its context. Let me explain.

Some students of James believe that 5.12 should stand alone, that it isn't related either to what comes before or what comes after it but is simply an important piece of instruction that James just sort of stuck in at this point. Others offer a variation of that:

Verse 12 has no immediate relation to its context but is part of James' general concern about the right use of the tongue, which goes all the way back to 3.1–12. Some of those who want to see the verse as attached to its context think it relates to verses 13–18, that James is saying we should pray and sing praises rather than swearing so he presents the negative first, then the positive. A fourth option seems most likely: Verse 12 relates more to what goes *before* it in verses 7–11. It is part of James' teaching on how to respond with patience when facing the hard times described in verses 1–6. That is, don't let life's stresses drive you to the use of oaths. Since we included verse 12 in our broader discussion of verses 7–11, that's obviously the view that I prefer. However, regardless what we decide about how the verse relates to the verses around it (if it does at all), its point is straightforward and simple: "Do not swear."

Not *That* Kind of Swearing

Before looking further at what James means by "Do not swear," we need to see what he *isn't* talking about, because there are two common misconceptions of his point.

First, he isn't talking about using profanity. That's certainly one type of swearing and obviously one Christians should avoid, but it isn't James' topic here. (See Eph 5.4 and Col 3.8 for Paul's prohibition of that kind of swearing.) James is talking about oath-taking, seeking to affirm one's word by saying such things as "by heaven" or "by earth." Unlike profanity, the issue here isn't the *kind* of words that are used but the *way* words are used.

Second, James isn't forbidding the taking of vows or solemn oaths. Many believers think he is and refuse to be sworn in during legal proceedings or to take solemn vows, but this misses the point. I should point out that this teaching doesn't originate with James but is his reflection on Jesus' own teachings in the Sermon on the Mount against the same kind of thing (Matt 5.33–37). Notice that Jesus ties the admonition against swearing at all to not swearing falsely—i.e., attesting to things you don't really mean and attempting to hide the deception by adding an oath ("By heaven"; "by earth"; "by Jerusalem").

But how do we know James and Jesus aren't also forbidding the taking of oaths on solemn occasions such as marriage, being sworn in during court proceedings, or the taking of religious vows? Simple. The Bible gives us numerous examples of these kinds of things being done, and they are not disapproved. For example, Deuteronomy 6.13 (and the parallel in Deut 10.10) says, "It is the Lord your God you shall fear. Him you shall serve and by his name you shall swear." According to Hebrews 6.13 and 17, God Himself took an oath when He made the covenant with Abraham. Likewise, Jesus allowed Himself to be placed under oath when He replied to the high priest concerning His identity as Messiah (Matt 26.63–64). Paul frequently affirmed his word by an oath, as in Philippians 1.8: "For God is my witness, how I yearn for you all with the affection of Christ Jesus," and Acts 18.18 reveals that Paul had taken something like the Nazirite vow described in Numbers 6, which must surely have involved placing oneself under a solemn oath to keep the vow. With all of that biblical precedent in mind, it becomes obvious that James isn't ruling out taking vows or allowing oneself to be placed under oath.

So What *Is* the Issue?

As noted earlier, it's really pretty simple: Christians are to be truthful people in everything we say and do, people who don't need to affirm what they say by an oath, because our word says it all. It's the same concern Jesus had in Matthew 5, in which He taught against not using phony oath-formulas to cover up the truth or to get out of doing whatever we promise to do or even thinking we can reinforce the truth by using an oath. The point is, simply let your word be sufficient.

It would be hard to imagine a teaching that's more practical, more relevant, or more needed in our own time than this one. Lying and cover-ups are so common we hardly know whom to believe any more. So many public officials and others in high places have been caught in lies that we have come to expect it rather than being shocked by it. People generally act so much out of self-interest that lying is just one of many tools to get what they want or to cover up the truth about what they did or why they did it. All of this prevarication makes us fearful and distrustful of one another, and it's hard to breathe in such a toxic moral atmosphere. We may even be tempted to join in the game out of a sense of self-preservation. We can certainly see this possibility in James' original setting, as his readers were suffering at the hands of unscrupulous people. Under such circumstances, why not just lie and use false oaths yourself in order to make life a little easier?

But James says an emphatic "No!" to such thinking. Literally, he says, "*Stop* swearing by heaven… " He knew it was going on and didn't want his readers to think it was okay—ever. As Jesus' words in the Sermon on the Mount demonstrate, such behavior simply isn't part of the ethics of God's Kingdom. God calls upon you and me to tell the truth at all times. And we certainly don't need to reinforce our words with empty oaths, since an oath adds nothing to the truth.

What's the Big Deal?

Still, we might wonder, why does James place such a premium on truth-telling and avoiding oaths when there are so many other moral and ethical issues that seem to be much more serious? Why not say, for instance, "But above all, my brothers, avoid sexual immorality," a topic he discusses not at all in this letter? Why is being truthful such a big deal? This is a reasonable question that deserves an answer.

First, we should be truthful because, to an honest person, swearing oaths in ordinary speech is absolutely useless and can cast doubt on our truthfulness. In reality "Yes" and "No" are all we need to say if we're telling the truth. Swearing "by" something adds nothing at all to the force of our words. In fact, Jesus says, "anything more comes from evil" (or "from the evil one"—Matt 5.37). Any time we resort to swearing oaths to persuade others that we're telling the truth, it's a sure sign there is an ulterior motive at work.

Second, swearing oaths presupposes that lying is the norm. I'm not talking about a "cultural" norm but our personal norm. If I add an oath to some of my words but not to others, what does that say about my oath-less words? Are they not equally true? What is it about the sworn words that makes them require an oath for reinforcement? In fact, the more someone swears to the truthfulness of their words, the more suspicious we ought to become. Why is so much oath-taking necessary to affirm they're telling the truth? And, if we likewise swear, people will begin to wonder about *us*, and that shouldn't be the case with believers.

Third, it's imperative to be truthful because you can't swear an oath without implicating God at some level. This is true whether we use His name or not. As His people, all we do and say is to be governed by His will, and if we swear an oath we imply we have God's approval to do so. If we use His name, as in a formal oath or vow, we had better mean and do what we say. Consider these sobering words:

> When you vow a vow to God, do not delay paying it, for he has no pleasure in fools. Pay what you vow. It is better that you should not vow than that you should vow and not pay. Let not

your mouth lead you into sin, and do not say before the messenger that it was a mistake. Why should God be angry at your voice and destroy the work of your hands? For when dreams increase and words grow many, there is vanity, but God is the one you must fear. (Eccl 5.4–7)

Granted, the words of Ecclesiastes 5 pertain specifically to a vow made *to* God, not one made to someone else while employing His name. Nevertheless, using God's name in this way implicates Him in the weakness of our words, and we have ample warning not to use His name in a "vain" (i.e., "empty") fashion (Exod 20.7). The warnings of the consequences of doing so are dire indeed, just as in James 5.12. Remember, the goal is "that you may not fall under condemnation."

While always speaking the truth might seem like a relatively small thing, it isn't. One simple way Christians can make a tremendous impact on our world is by being truthful people, because truthfulness is such a rare quality. If you always speak the truth, even when it places you at a disadvantage, you will without doubt stand out from the crowd. And by doing so you will reflect the truthful character of the God you worship and will give people an added reason to listen when you tell them anything, but especially when you tell them "the word of truth, the gospel" (Col 1.5).

Dear Lord and Father of mankind,
Forgive our foolish ways;
Reclothe us in our rightful mind,
In purer lives Thy service find,
In deeper rev'rence praise.

John G. Whittier, "Dear Lord and Father of Mankind"

"And the prayer of faith will save the one who is sick,
and the Lord will raise him up." (5.13–18)

3/15/2015

SEVENTEEN | *Faith Healing*
or Healing Faith?

?, → Have

How you ever noticed that when a biblical text is *abused* by one group, it tends to be *neglected* by others? An obvious example is the Book of Revelation. Because it has for so long been used as a playground for all kinds of weird theories about the "end-times," most folks who don't buy into those theories tend not to read it much at all. For some reason, we naturally avoid that which others have obscured, rather than working to come to a clearer understanding.

James 5.13–18 is such a text. As you're probably well aware, this paragraph has been abused by those popularly referred to as "faith healers," people who believe they have some divine gift to bring healing to others. Such people believe they possess the same gift of healing which Jesus had and which He bestowed on the apostles and which survived at least for a while in the early church. Such a misunderstanding is regrettable enough, but it seldom stops there. The focus of the "ministries" of such self-proclaimed healers (who authenticates or certifies them?) becomes the act of healing itself, not the proclamation of the gospel of Christ. As a result, that which was adjunct to the ministry of Jesus and the apostles becomes the headline, while the true story of Jesus' sacrificial death and the salvation He brings is relegated to a note somewhere on page two—or maybe even further away. In addition, there is always the temptation to parlay these supposed powers into financial gain (and fame) for the healer, while holding out a false hope to people who are already suffering desperately.

One common claim among such healers is that people will be healed only if they have "enough faith." This excuse covers any and all failures on their part: anyone not healed simply didn't have "enough faith" (as though there is some prescribed biblical "amount" of faith necessary for the power of God to kick in). As a result, when they don't experience healing, suffering people are left feeling that they are also somehow spiritually defective.

It isn't hard to see why James 5.13–18 attracts these folks. It has all the necessary elements for a dramatic "healing service": the anointing with oil, confession of sin, prayer, and praise. So there is the tendency to see this text as describing exactly what faith healers claim to do.

Because of that, James 5.13–18 tends to be neglected by the rest of us, who reject that sort of faith healing based on biblical evidence but who may not be exactly sure just what James *is* talking about. We're uncertain whether he's describing a miraculous healing or not, and if not, whether calling the elders together to anoint with oil is something we should still do. So we tend to just leave it alone, which is a shame. Not only is it a great text with an important message, but it's also James' last major paragraph in the letter before signing off. Obviously, if we ignore this text, we're missing out on something important, something God wants us to know and do. Let's see if we can determine what that something is.

Beware of Easy Answers. . .

In all fairness to the various interpretations of James 5.13–18 and to the tendency to neglect it, the text does raise some thorny questions which are not easily answered. So we need to at least attempt an answer to these.

1. Does James 5.13–18 describe an incident of spiritual or physical healing? And, if it's a physical healing, is it miraculous in nature?

These questions arise primarily because of verse 15a: "And the prayer of faith will save the one who is sick, and the Lord will raise him up." The word for "save" is *sozo,* the common New Testament word for spiritual salvation, and the word for "raise…up" *(egeiro)* is the usual term for someone's being raised from the dead. This raises the possibility that James might not be writing about a physical healing at all but rather about someone being "healed" spiritually, "saved" from their sins and "raised up" to new life in Christ. It's tempting to opt for this interpretation, since it would then steal some thunder from the faith healers.

However, this doesn't seem likely. For one thing, James speaks of someone who is "sick" (v 14), not someone who is "lost." In addition the rest of verse 15 argues against the "spiritual healing" interpretation: "And *if* he has committed sins, he will be forgiven." The forgiveness of the subject's sins seems to be a separate (but related) topic from that of his healing. In fact, forgiveness may not be involved at all, as indicated by the word "if." It seems likely that what we have here is a reference to physical healing—but not to a "faith healing." Notice that the "elders" of the church are to be summoned, not some specially gifted healer (unless the healer also claims to be an elder), and they are to anoint the sick person and pray, not exercise some miraculous gift.

2. Why call for the elders, and what is the point of anointing the sick person with oil?

Let's think first about the oil. In the Bible anointing someone with oil can have one of two purposes. First is the medicinal use of oil, as in Luke 10.34 when the Good Samaritan "poured on oil and wine." Apparently these were the only healing substances he had with him (a sort of First-Century "first aid kit"), and the oil would provide some soothing and the wine a bit of antiseptic for the injured man's wounds. Given the undeveloped state of medicine in the First Century AD, these must have been common home remedies, and it isn't surprising to find them in use in Luke 10, nor would it be in James 5. We should note, however, that the only other New Testament text to connect oil with healing is Mark 6.13, which says the apostles anointed the sick with oil as they healed them, but it is questionable whether or not we should understand the use of oil as medicinal in that context. More likely it belongs with the other common use of oil in Scripture, as a symbol of the presence of God's Spirit, particularly in circumstances where someone is healed by the power of God's Spirit or chosen for some special service, as in the case of the anointing of Israelite kings and priests. (See 1 Sam 10.1, 16.1, 12–13, and Exod 30.22–33 for examples of the latter.) Oil could also be poured on someone's head simply as a sign of God's blessing or as a means of bestowing honor, but the basic symbolism of the presence of the Spirit seems to be the same (Psa 23.5; Luke 7.44–47).

So how is the oil being used in James 5? While it's impossible to rule out the medicinal usage here, it seems more likely symbolic. If it were simply for medicinal purposes, anyone could have applied it and there would have been no need to call the elders. Likewise, James specifies the "prayer of faith" will save the sick person, not the application of oil. So the oil is most likely a symbol of the Spirit's blessing and healing of the sick person, which helps explain why the sick person is to call the elders. While both of these acts could apparently be done by anyone, the elders would be men of spiritual maturity who were known to be men of prayer. Some students of this text suggest that the elders are the ones most likely to be in possession of miraculous spiritual gifts such as healing, but notice that James focuses not on their powers but on their prayers. Also, the idea of elders being more likely to have spiritual gifts is difficult to maintain in light of texts such as 1 Corinthians 12.11, which suggests the bestowal of spiritual gifts is somewhat random (the Spirit "apportions to each one individually as he wills") and not tied to any particular role or function in the church.

3. Is the healing of the sick person guaranteed by this text?

Another way to put this question is, can a sick person take James 5.13–18 as a *promise* of healing if the proper procedures are followed? Are the faith healers right when they say, "Name it and claim it"—simply accept this promise at face value, and healing will be yours (again, *if* you have enough faith)?

The answer to this one should be relatively clear: No. Nothing in the Bible ever indicates that healing is "guaranteed." While the example of Jesus healing the multitudes is frequently cited as proof that trusting souls can have healing if they only believe, there is more to the story than that. First, while Jesus did heal many, He didn't heal everyone, not even everyone who sought Him out for healing. Texts such as Mark 1.32–34 indicate that Jesus healed "many," but they don't say He healed everyone. And several times the Gospels record Jesus withdrawing from the crowds to go by Himself to pray, leaving them clamoring for His presence and, no doubt, for more healing (Mark 6.45–56). Although it is sometimes claimed that one of Jesus' purposes in coming to earth was to heal everyone, this is not the case according to the Gospels. If Jesus had wanted to heal everyone, He could readily have done so merely by proclaiming the whole world to be healed. That He never did this indicates that healing was part of a larger purpose of proclaiming the kingdom of God, not a primary end in itself.

In addition we have several examples in Scripture of people who desired healing but didn't receive it. Paul, in writing about his "thorn in the flesh," says, "Three times I pleaded with the Lord about this, that it should leave me. But he said to me, 'My grace is sufficient for you, for my power is made perfect in weakness'" (2 Cor 12.8–9). Even such a faithful servant as Paul didn't receive the healing he sought, which should put to rest the idea that those not healed "just don't have enough faith." Also, Paul didn't heal Timothy of his stomach ailments (1 Tim 5.23), and rather than healing his co-worker Trophimus, 2 Tim 4.20 says he "left [him] ill at Miletus," even though the Book of Acts shows that Paul did at times exercise healing powers (14.1–10, etc.). Also, there is nothing in James 5 that suggests that "God wants everyone well" or that physical healing is central to the gospel message.

Why then does James speak so absolutely in verse 15? He seems to leave little room for doubt that the sick will be healed under the circumstances he describes. This absoluteness leads many to conclude that James must be talking about *miraculous* healing in which the results are guaranteed. This may in fact be the case, but we should note that even in the case of those who clearly possessed such gifts, healing still wasn't always a sure thing, as in Luke 9.37–43. Perhaps the key lies in the expression "the prayer of faith." Jesus taught us in His prayer in the garden that faithful prayer in its truest sense always includes "if it be your will." It is never an attempt to bind God to the doing of our own wills but always the submission of ours to His. In that case, even a prayer for healing will acknowledge that, for some reason unknown to us and perhaps beyond our understanding, healing may not be God's will, a dilemma we will explore in the next chapter. Perhaps we should think of what James describes here as the norm for prayer for healing, with the full realization that there always may be exceptions.

4. What is the connection between sickness and sin?

The second part of verse 15 raises this issue, since James adds, "If he has committed sins, he will be forgiven." While it seems unlikely that James assumes that all sickness is a result of sin (note the "if"), he also recognizes the possibility that it may be. That sickness can be caused by sin not only is obvious from human experience and observation (for example, the effects of alcoholism, drug addiction, or excessive eating) but is also confirmed in John 5.14, where Jesus tells the once-lame man to "Sin no more, that nothing worse may happen to you." But even if someone seeking healing has an illness not caused by sin, there may still be the need for confession. If the person isn't right with God, an appeal for physical healing is out of order; he needs to take care of first things first by confessing sin, then seek to be healed.

[handwritten margin note: I disagree! The healing may actually be on his Road to recovery of his sin.]

...And Don't Miss the Point

While all of these questions are interesting and important, we may not be able to come up with completely satisfactory answers. However, that shouldn't distract us from the central message of this great text. For in the final analysis, this isn't a text about healing *per se* or the proper circumstances for bringing it about. It's primarily *a paragraph on prayer*, which is mentioned no less than seven times in these six verses. Healing is only one circumstance which might call forth prayer, but the subject is prayer itself. What do we learn about it here?

1. First, James 5.13–18 teaches us to react spiritually to all of our circumstances, whether good or bad.

Notice that there are at least four types of circumstances discussed in this text: suffering (generally, not necessarily physically, since illness is mentioned later), cheerfulness, illness, and being guilty of sin. James says, in every circumstance, respond in a spiritual way. The sufferer should respond to her trials by praying. The cheerful person should sing praise. After all, we shouldn't look to God only when in trouble, but should praise Him when things are going well. The sick person should call for the elders and have them anoint with oil and pray. It's part of their pastoral (shepherding) responsibility to see to the needs of the sick but especially to minister to them spiritually. So while they're at it, they can also pray for the sick person's sins, if that's part of the problem. (On the other hand, when is sin *not* part of our problems?)

So the lesson is, look to God in all circumstances, good or bad, and utilize the resources of Christian leaders, prayer, confession, praise, and whatever else might be appropriate.

2. Second, the power of prayer is limitless, so we should pray boldly.

Notice how many people James mentions as praying in verses 13–18: the sufferer, the elders, the Christian confessing sin, and "the righteous person," with the great prophet Elijah as the prime example of what praying should be like.

Verse 16b is the primary statement about prayer, with Elijah serving as the model. "The prayer of a righteous person has great power as it is working." Those who pray, James has already said and now says again, should pray with the conviction that God is both willing and able to answer prayer (see 1.5–8). "The righteous person" is not necessarily a "super-righteous" person but rather the one who truly seeks God and His will. Then comes the example of Elijah with a specific reference to 1 Kings 17–18, where Elijah confronted the evil king Ahab with the disciplining power of God. He declared to Ahab that it would not rain, and for three years it didn't. Later he prayed again for God to break the drought, and He did. James says Elijah prayed "fervently," not half-heartedly or casually. When we want something from God, we should apply ourselves to prayer, not giving up and not being afraid to ask for what we desire. The remarkable thing about Elijah's prayer is its specific nature: he prayed for no rain and then for rain, and the rains left and returned on cue, leaving no doubt as to the activity of God. This was no vague, anemic prayer but a bold, specific one. And Elijah was, James reminds us, "a man with a nature like ours," so there's no reason we can't pray as he did.

Why are we so often hesitant in prayer? It may be simply a lack of faith, but there are often other reasons. For example, we are sometimes in a quandary about praying for the sick. Is it okay to ask for healing, especially for ourselves? Are we being selfish in doing so (remembering what James said in 4.3 about selfish praying)? Are we attempting to impose our wills on God? Would a faithful person simply take whatever comes and trust in God, rather than seeking a different outcome? The truth is, we don't know God's will about such things, but His word teaches us to bring our requests to Him and let Him sort out what is best and right. Isn't that what Paul was saying in Philippians 4.6 when he wrote, "...do not be anxious about anything, but in everything by prayer and supplication with thanksgiving let your requests be made known to God"? If it's something that might cause us anxiety—whether our health or something else—it's something about which we should pray.

There's little question that we need bolder praying in the church today than what we usually do. We should pray boldly for the sick, for the lost, for the unfaithful, for deliverance from trouble, for guidance, and for the progress of the church. If James 5.13-18 teaches us anything, it teaches us to ask and ask boldly!

So James 5.13-18 isn't a text in support of faith-healing. But it is a text about healing faith, the faith that causes us to look to

God, and to beseech Him boldly for whatever concerns us, believing that He can and will give what is best.

> *When life's dark maze I tread,*
> *And griefs around me spread,*
> *Be thou my guide;*
> *Bid darkness turn to day,*
> *Wipe sorrow's tears away,*
> *Nor let me ever stray*
> *From Thee aside.*

Ray Palmer, "My Faith Looks Up to Thee"

"The prayer of a righteous person has great power as it is working." (5.13–18)

3/22

EIGHTEEN | *When Healing Doesn't Happen*

Few circumstances in life pull at our hearts like the serious illness of someone we love or shake us to our core as much as when we are the one who is ill. So it isn't surprising that we tend to cling to a verse like James 5.15 when it promises, "And the prayer of faith will save the one who is sick, and the Lord will raise him up." It sounds so absolute, so positively hopeful.

Yet you and I know it doesn't always happen that way. We pray and pray, boldly asking for God's healing of ourselves or someone we love, but the illness remains or worsens, and often death comes instead of healing. We know God can heal, that Jesus healed many, and that Paul and Peter healed. And James encourages us to pray like Elijah and have others pray for us, knowing that "the prayer of a righteous person has great power as it is working." And still healing doesn't always happen.

Yes, there are many times when it does happen, and we're always so thankful for those blessings. But that only makes us wonder all the more: why does it happen sometimes and not others? In those instances when healing doesn't happen, is there something wrong with our faith? With our prayers? We're afraid even to think it, but sometimes we do: has there been some failure on God's part? Is this just a situation even He couldn't handle? Is He, as Harold Kushner suggests in *When Bad Things Happen to Good People*, all-knowing and all-loving, but *not* all-powerful, a benevolent Father who would help us if He could but just can't? Does He, too, stand anxiously by, desperately wanting to help but with His hands just as tied as ours?

I will tell you quickly that I don't have all the answers to the questions of why healing sometimes happens and sometimes doesn't. But I'm persuaded that God's word offers us help in thinking about this, and it encourages us to trust God, even when—perhaps *especially* when—healing doesn't happen.

These Aren't the Answer

If we're going to think clearly (and biblically) about these questions, there are some ideas we need to get rid of once and for all. As stated in Chapter Seventeen, some of these ideas are fostered by the "faith-healers" who claim powers they don't really have as a way of giving themselves an "out" when they fail. But the problem is not who teaches these things, it's that these ideas are themselves not taught in Scripture. So let's be clear at the start about what we need to toss out.

First, it simply isn't true that "God desires everyone to be well" and that "Jesus came to banish sickness from the earth." If this were so, there would be no sickness at all. Jesus could have eradicated all illness simply by commanding it. In fact, God the Father could have done so without His Son ever having to come to earth; He could have declared by divine fiat that everyone should be made well and stay that way. But that isn't what happened. And when Jesus was on the earth, He didn't heal everyone, nor did His servants Peter and Paul and the other apostles. There was a "gift" of healing in the early church (1 Cor 7.9), but even with that people still got sick and not all got well. So Scripture does not support this claim and clearly contradicts it.

Second, the corollary to this is, the Bible never says that if people don't get well, even after prayer and anointing, it's a sign of a lack of or weakness in faith. Let's consider the example of the blind man Jesus healed in John 9. After Jesus gave this man, who had never seen in his life, the gift of sight, he became something of a "religious issue" to the local Pharisees. Who did this? Why was it done on the Sabbath? Was the man ever really blind to begin with? What did his parents have to say about him? If Jesus were an evil-doer, how could He possibly have done such a God-empowered thing as to restore someone's sight, Sabbath or not? When the dust had settled a bit, Jesus sought out the formerly-sightless man. He may have become little more than an enigma to the Pharisees, but to Jesus he was still a man made in God's image and needed to be ministered to further. When Jesus found him He asked, "Do you believe in the Son of Man?" Now watch the man's reply: "And who is he, sir, that I may believe in him?" Jesus then proclaimed, "You have seen him, and it is he who is speaking to you." Only then did the man announce, "Lord, I believe," and then worshiped Jesus (John 9.35–38). Notice: the man had been fully healed, yet he had no idea who Jesus was. His healing was purely an act of Christ's power, not the product of his faith. God doesn't need our faith in order to work His will.

A parallel incident further bears this out. In Acts 3.1–10 Peter and John encountered a lame man lying at the "Beautiful Gate" of the temple, begging for handouts from those who entered. Peter offered him no money but something far better: "In the name of Jesus Christ of Nazareth, rise up and walk!" In response the man not only walked, but jumped up from where he was and praised God for his healing. There was nothing conditional about what Peter did or said to the man. He didn't say, "If you believe strongly enough, if you name it and claim it, then you can be healed."

[handwritten margin note: nothing recorded]

Rather, he commanded him to walk in Jesus' name, and the man did. Some will point to verse 16 to suggest the man walked only because he believed: "And his name—by faith in his name—has made this man strong whom you see and know, and the faith that is through Jesus has given the man this perfect health in the presence of you all." But the record of the event itself shows it wasn't the lame man's faith that made him well, but the faith of the apostles. If faith on the part of the lame man were a prerequisite for his healing, why wasn't he told that? Again, the claim simply isn't true. Sometimes people aren't healed, and it has nothing at all to do with their lack of faith.

Consider This…

I fully realize that, by debunking these false claims, I haven't answered the question of why healing sometimes doesn't happen. Believe me, if I had the answer, I would state it outright in as few words as possible—but I don't. What I do offer is some thoughts from Scripture to help us get our minds around this conundrum and help us think it through faithfully. None of these is "the answer" either, but bear with me and see if this helps.

1. *God has the power to do anything He wills to do.* Nothing could be more emphatically stated in Scripture than this great truth: God is all-powerful. Remember when the three "men" (at least two of whom turn out to be angels of the Lord—Gen 19.1) first visited Abraham and Sarah to confirm to them God's promise of a son who was to be born within a year (Gen 18.10)? Because she was "worn out" and Abraham was so old, Sarah laughed to herself when she heard the news (18.12–13). And who could blame her, given the circumstances? But the Lord (apparently speaking through one of the men) said, "Is anything too hard for the Lord?" (18.14), and the obvious answer is, "Of course not!" And eventually Sarah had a baby. Jesus later stated the same truth positively

by asserting, "...with God all things are possible" (Matt 19.26). Paul takes the thought even further by declaring that God is able to do "far more abundantly than all that we ask or think" (Eph 3.20). So whatever the explanation for our lack of healing, the answer doesn't lie in any limitations on God's part. We can imagine being made well; that's something God can obviously do.

So why does God sometimes not heal? It must be the case that somehow our healing doesn't fall within the parameters of His will. I realize this calls for even greater trust in God on our part. The reason Kushner opts for the view that "God would if He could, but He can't" is because it's easier to accept that than to accept that God *can* but, for some reason unknown to us, He won't. It may be easier to believe in a handicapped God, but Scripture won't allow it and challenges us instead to trust what we cannot possibly understand.

Here's where our practice of praying "if it be Thy will" really gets put to the test! Are we *really* ready to accept God's will? Do we trust Him *that* much, when our lives or the lives of those we love are at stake? It may be much harder, but it's far more biblical than Kushner's solution.

2. *God takes no delight in the suffering of His children.* In Matthew 10.24–31 Jesus sought to prepare His disciples for the reality that they must suffer and be rejected just as He was about to be. He reassured them by saying that not even a sparrow (monetarily worth only half a penny!) falls to the ground "apart from your Father," then declaring, "Fear not, therefore; you are of more value than many sparrows." If God is involved even in the death of a sparrow (and note that He doesn't keep them from falling), He is certainly involved in the suffering of His human children. That means when you suffer and healing doesn't happen, God is involved in that experience with you and is there to provide a

constant source of strength and even of peace about what you're going through. So rather than turn our backs on God in the midst of suffering, we have all the more reason to pray—and remember, that's James' main point in 5.15–18. "Is anyone among you suffering? Let him pray."

God will not leave you without resources to cope with your suffering and loss. If you pray and pray and healing doesn't happen, then pray for strength to endure and for peace to accept it. God will grant one or the other, if not both.

3. *God sometimes uses sickness to accomplish His purposes in us.* That God can work through something as negative as illness or even death itself to accomplish positive ends is a testimony to His incredible power. And we know that has to be true because of the Cross where Jesus died, the greatest possible example of good resulting from bad. Isaiah 53 vividly describes the suffering and rejection the Servant of the Lord would endure for the sins of others, yet the same chapter declares,

> When his soul makes an offering for guilt,
> he shall see his offspring; he shall prolong his days;
> the will of the Lord shall prosper in his hand.
> Out of the anguish of his soul he shall see and be satisfied;
> by his knowledge shall the righteous one, my servant, make
>   many to be
> accounted righteous, and he shall bear their iniquities.

Paul learned this lesson through his own suffering. Second Corinthians 12.7–10 records his petition (offered three times) that God would remove his "thorn in the flesh," the "messenger of Satan" sent to harass him. Surely, Paul must have reasoned, it would be God's will to remove this thorn so he could serve even more fully and effectively in proclaiming Christ to the Gentiles. He must have been somewhat taken aback by the Lord's reply: "My grace is sufficient for you, for my power is made perfect in weakness." Did you get that? God's power is not made perfect through our strength or our success or our happiness, but through our weakness. When we are most helpless, that's when God's power really shines through. As a result, Paul realized that the "thorn" (whatever it was) served a dual purpose: (1) It kept him humble, as a constant reminder of his frailty and that it was only by God's power and grace that he was able to serve Him at all. (2) It showed him that the true path to spiritual power lay not in his strengths and successes but in his weaknesses, of which he then learned to "boast" rather than boasting about himself. Granted, it's a hard way to learn these lessons, but sometimes we're hard to teach.

Yet another example comes from that man born blind in John 9. When Jesus' disciples first encountered the man, they, like the Pharisees, treated him as something of a "case study." "Who sinned," they asked, "this man or his parents, that he was born blind?" In other words, who do we blame for this situation and all others like it? What's the theological explanation for someone being "punished" from the womb? Was it the fault of his parents (easy enough to imagine) or perhaps his own fault (yes, pre-natal sin!)? Jesus said it was neither, "but that the works of God might be displayed in him" (9.3). Let me hasten to point out that this *doesn't* mean "God made him blind all his life so He could get glory from his eventual healing." Rather, as F. F. Bruce commented, "God overruled the disaster of the child's blindness so that, when the child grew to manhood, he might, by recovering his sight, see the glory of God in the face of Christ." God isn't in the business of making people blind (or sick or poor or abused). Those things happen as the result of living in a fallen, sinful world. But when healing doesn't happen, it *may be* that God wants to do some-

[handwritten margin note: OT says otherwise — Ex 4:11]

[handwritten note at bottom: so blindness comes from sin?]

thing in us or through us, or teach us something that can only be accomplished or learned through affliction.

Hannah More, an 18th-Century poet and dramatist, suffered much in her later years from respiratory illness but developed an ever-deepening spiritual life in the process. She wrote,

> Affliction is the school in which great virtues are acquired and in which great characters are formed. It is like a spiritual gymnasium in which the disciples of Christ are trained in robust exercise, hardy exertion and severe conflict. We do not hear of military heroes in peacetime, nor of the most distinguished saints in the quiet and unmolested periods of church history. The courage in the warrior and the devotion in the saint continue to survive, ready to be brought into action when perils beset the country or trials assail the Church, but it must be admitted that in long periods of inaction both are susceptible to decay.

I should hasten to add that this isn't the same as saying that suffering is the result of sin or that when affliction or illness comes it's because God needs to root something out of us. Sometimes suffering does result from sin, but the point is, even when that's not the case, God may choose to work through your illness to help you grow spiritually in ways you never would if all were well. And whether or not that's what is happening in someone's life is between them and God. It isn't for others to judge or try to explain. When you find yourself tempted to offer an "explanation" of someone else's suffering, put your hand over your mouth, because the truth is you don't know why this is happening. But God does, and that's what matters.

4. *Ultimate healing is not to be found in this life.* Think about it: Even if God does grant healing, you will be sick again and will at some point die. It's going to happen to all of us. We frequently

forget that all of those people the Gospels record as being healed by Jesus eventually died, and so will we all. That doesn't at all mean that relief from suffering now isn't a worthy desire or something to pray about. After all, that's why James says what he does in 5.13–18. What it does mean is that we also need a higher goal than healing. When Paul told the Philippians that he knew his imprisonment would "turn out for my deliverance" (Phil 1.19), he didn't necessarily mean getting out of jail. Verse 20 makes that clear, as Paul says, "now as always Christ will be honored in my body, whether by life or by death." In other words, "deliverance" for Paul could mean being set free by means of death from his earthly labors and suffering.

Revelation 21.1–4 promises that God will someday abolish sickness and even death itself. *That* is our ultimate healing: our salvation through Jesus Christ. Everything else pales in comparison. So when healing doesn't happen, it may mean that God is moving us toward a far greater blessing. That may be hard to accept, but when we do accept it, it gives us an entirely new perspective on the whole issue of being healed—or not being healed. It also causes us to pray differently. I've often been asked by the grieving loved one of a Christian who is suffering and near death if it's okay to pray that they'll just be able to go on and be with the Lord. There's a certain amount of guilt that almost always goes with praying that someone will die. But how could it *not* be okay? Praying in that way simply means we trust the promises God has made for that person, as well as for ourselves.

Back to the Question...
Returning to our original question about James 5.15 and its absoluteness, how should we understand this verse, if it isn't promising that God will heal all of those for whom we pray? Here's my suggestion: I think James 5.15 tells us what often *will* happen

when we pray, unless God has something else in mind, which is beyond our ability to know. And when healing doesn't happen? Two suggestions: Keep praying. The healing we desire, or perhaps even something better, may come about yet. And keep trusting. Trust in a loving heavenly Father who knows and cares about your every pain and every concern. And be thankful that your life is in His hands.

> *Ye fearful saints, fresh courage take, The clouds ye so much dread*
> *Are big with mercy, and shall break In blessings on your head.*
> *His purposes will ripen fast, Unfolding ev'ry hour;*
> *The bud may have a bitter taste, But sweet will be the flower.*

William Cowper, "God Moves in a Mysterious Way"

"...whoever brings back a sinner from the error of his wandering will save his soul from death." (5.19–20)

NINETEEN | *Saving Souls from Death*

So This Is a Letter?

All through this study I've been referring to "the Letter of James." That's what it's called in the headings of most Bibles, and James is usually classified as one of the "General Letters" (or "Epistles") of the New Testament. And for good reason, since it starts out very much like what we expect in an ancient letter: "James, a servant of God and of the Lord Jesus Christ, To the twelve tribes in the Dispersion. Greetings." Compare this to any of the letters of Paul and you'll see something similar.

However, when we get to the end of James, the letter form suddenly evaporates, and it ends somewhat abruptly and without any epistolary "signing off." It just stops. In addition, many would say it ends somewhat off topic, with James going off on a subject he hasn't discussed previously but wanted to stick in there before he ended the letter: the need to bring back from their "wandering" those who have "wandered from the truth." All of this makes us wonder if what we call "the Letter of James" was originally a letter at all. If not, what else might it have been? Very likely a sermon or what we might think of as a "tract," a kind of topical essay on the theme of wise living for dispossessed believers. That would make sense, since the address and greeting at the beginning could have been added as a way of addressing the message to an audience of churches in a particular locale. But it's also possible (and seems more likely) that James knew to whom he wanted to address this written sermon, so he started out as though writing a letter and ended it as he would a sermon.

So much for the non-letter ending and its apparent abruptness. But what about the idea that James has gone off topic in the process? That doesn't seem to be quite accurate for three reasons. First, all through the letter James has been writing about wisdom, covering everything from how to endure trials to how to treat the poor to how to get along in the church. In the final two verses he discusses restoring to the faith those who have wandered away from it. What could be wiser than that? If, as James says, people's souls are in jeopardy and we have the capacity to do something about it, isn't what he says in verses 19–20 simply more wisdom teaching? Second, it's hard to argue that James has suddenly gone off topic when he has just completed a paragraph in which he discusses prayer both for the sick and for those who have committed sins. "Wandering from the truth" is certainly a particular kind of sin, so it seems that rather than switching topics, James has moved on to an extension of the topic at hand, something his readers need to pray about. Third, one of James' primary concerns in the letter is the endurance of trials and the testing of one's faith, with the obvious recognition that under such circumstances, some will succumb to temptation and wander from the faith. James has been calling his readers to action from the outset, so what better way to end the letter than by encouraging his readers to bring those people back who have wandered away?

Yes, It Can Happen!

Something that hinders a proper understanding of James' last two verses is the idea that wandering from the truth to the point of becoming spiritually lost simply isn't possible. This belief goes by many titles: "Eternal security of the believer," "once-saved-always-saved," and "the impossibility of apostasy," to name just a few. The idea is that once a person becomes a born-again believer in Christ, falling away simply isn't possible, that one of the blessings of being in Christ is the security of knowing that no matter what happens (or, as some say, even what you do or don't do) you can never lose the blessing of salvation. For many this belief is part of a larger doctrinal view that says God has pre-determined those who will be saved, so naturally it isn't possible for them to be lost. For others it isn't so much a matter of systematic theology as of finding comfort in the idea that they can never lose what has been gained in Christ, so they latch onto it as an article of faith.

Problem is, James says it *is* possible. In fact, he assumes that it will happen in some cases and that believers who don't wander off need to be prepared to bring back those who do. Let's look at his statement phrase-by-phrase:

"My brothers." The reference obviously is to *Christian* brothers. Some, in trying to avoid the conclusion that James is teaching the possibility of falling away, argue that "brothers" means "brothers" in the usual Jewish sense, something like "neighbors," but not in the Christian sense of being in spiritual fellowship. This has some merit, since James is a letter steeped in Jewish thought, as we've observed. However, James 2.1 argues against this conclusion, since there James speaks to "my brothers" in the context of a Christian worship assembly. Likewise, it's hard to believe he would speak to his readers as "my brothers" in the Jewish sense in 3.1, since the subject is who should and who shouldn't teach. This

is a discussion for the Christian community only. So in the last two verses of his letter, James is addressing his Christian brothers.

"If any one among you." If the "brothers" addressed are fellow-Christians, then this could only refer to someone numbered among them. So James is talking about the reclaiming of wandering Christians, not about the evangelism of non-believers.

"Wanders from the truth." This "truth" to which James refers is a comprehensive term, including both what Christians believe and how they live. "Wandering" from it would involve a departure in either the doctrinal or the ethical/moral realm. For James the two are inseparable, as clearly stated in 2.14–26. Again, this can only refer to Christians who have wandered from the faith, since it's impossible to "wander from" some place you've never been.

"Saves his soul from death." The death of one's soul is nothing other than the loss of salvation, and it's just playing games with the text to try to make it say anything else.

In addition, there is ample testimony from elsewhere in Scripture to show that falling (or wandering) away from Christ and losing one's salvation is certainly possible. Remember Jesus' "Parable of the Sower" (Matt 13.1–9)? In his explanation of the various types of soil (representing human hearts and their reaction to the "word of the kingdom"), Jesus said, "As for what was sown on rocky ground, this is the one who hears the word and immediately receives it with joy, yet he has no root in himself, but endures for a while, and when tribulation or persecution arises on account of the word, immediately he falls away" (13.21). According to Jesus some people do indeed hear the word and receive it but later "fall away." As a result, they bear no fruit. Notice that those who represent "good soil" bear fruit in various measures, depending on the individual and perhaps other circumstances, but the other kinds of soil (people) bear none at all.

When Paul wrote to the Galatians, they were in danger of attaching their hopes to something other than the gospel by relying on works of the law (especially circumcision) to bring them salvation. Speaking as emphatically as possible, Paul says in 5.2–4, "Look: I, Paul, say to you that if you accept circumcision, Christ will be of no advantage to you. I testify again to every man who accepts circumcision that he is obligated to keep the whole law. You are severed from Christ, you who would be justified by the law; you have fallen away from grace." Notice in 1.2 that this letter is addressed "to the churches of Galatia," so there is no question that Paul is speaking to Christians. Some of these Christians, he says, have "fallen away from grace" so Christ was no longer of any advantage to them—exactly what so many say cannot possibly happen.

Perhaps the strongest argument of all against the idea of eternal-security-regardless is the book of Hebrews. The letter (which, like James, seems to have originated as a sermon) warns Jewish Christians not to revert to their former religious system based on inadequate sacrifices but encourages them to continue to follow Christ. Interspersed throughout the letter are warnings of the consequences of turning back. The first comes in 2.1 when the writer says, "Therefore we must pay the closer attention to what we have heard, lest we drift away from it." He then asks, "How shall we escape if we neglect such a great salvation?" (2.3), and the obvious implied answer is "We won't!" Likewise, 3.12 speaks of believers "falling away from the living God." How could anyone do that and still be saved? Amazingly, some expositors of Hebrews strain so hard to insist that falling away isn't possible that they say that all of these warning passages are merely hypothetical, that no one can actually fall away but, if they could, these would be the consequences. How sad that in attempting to defend their view of salvation these people declare such a low view of Scripture.

One last example: In 1 Corinthians 9.24–27 Paul writes of the need for discipline and self-control in living the Christian life, comparable to that required of athletes. Toward the end of that paragraph he writes, "So I do not run aimlessly; I do not box as one beating the air. But I discipline my body and keep it under control, lest after preaching to others I myself should be disqualified." "Disqualified" from what? From what he offered to others through the preaching of the gospel: eternal life. Paul fully realized that, even as an apostle of Christ, he must discipline himself to live as God directed or risk losing the salvation so freely given to him.

What Paul says about himself is true of all of us. We are never so holy or spiritual that we are incapable of falling away. So James 5.19–20 serves the dual function of challenging faithful believers to seek and reclaim wanderers and warning them not to become one. The consequences are far too serious.

Now the Good News

It isn't the primary function of verses 19–20 to teach that people can fall away and be lost; that fact is assumed. Rather, the main purpose is to say that, by God's grace, it's possible for wanderers to be brought back and that Christians (all) have a responsibility to make bringing them back a priority. Not that this idea is anything new, for as far back as the book of Ezekiel the Bible says,

> And you, son of man, say to the house of Israel, Thus have you said: 'Surely our transgressions and our sins are upon us, and we rot away because of them. How then can we live?' Say to them, As I live, declares the Lord God, I have no pleasure in the death of the wicked, but that the wicked turn from his way and live; turn back, turn back from your evil ways, for why will you die, O house of Israel? (Ezek 33.10–11)

According to this text, it is inherent in God's nature to desire back that which belongs to Him, and so He offers sinners the opportunity to return and be forgiven, exactly what James 5.19–20 is about. The decision to turn away from God and to stay away is always ours, never His, for He has "no pleasure in the death of the wicked."

Earlier we noted that Hebrews contains all of those "warning passages" about the danger of falling away. In regard to sinners always being able to return to the Lord, one of these is particularly troubling. Hebrews 5 and 6 urge followers of Christ to press on in becoming mature in the faith and not be content with merely the "milk" of the word and the elementary doctrines of the faith. Then comes this dire warning:

> For it is impossible to restore again to repentance those who have once been enlightened, who have tasted the heavenly gift, and have shared in the Holy Spirit, and have tasted the goodness of the word of God and the powers of the age to come, if they then fall away, since they are crucifying once again the Son of God to their own harm and holding him up to contempt. For land that has drunk the rain that often falls on it, and produces a crop useful to those for whose sake it is cultivated, receives a blessing from God. But if it bears thorns and thistles, it is worthless and near to being cursed, and its end is to be burned. (Heb 6.4–8)

Return with me to our passage in James. It should be noted that James is clearly speaking about saved people who fall away. There is simply no other way to understand his description of a person who has "once been enlightened" and "tasted the heavenly gift" and "shared in the Holy Spirit" and who has "tasted the goodness of the word of God and the powers of the age to come." That such people can fall away we have already seen in several other texts. What is different is the troubling statement that it is "impossible" for such people to be restored when they fall away. In what sense is it "impossible," and, if it is impossible, why should we bother to do what James says in 5.19–20, since it won't do any good? Taking both Hebrews 6.4 and James 5.19–20 into account, we must conclude that there are some who have so rejected the faith they once held that they are beyond hope. However, this doesn't mean this is always the case. Hebrews may be describing an especially recalcitrant form of apostasy, a vigorous denial of Christ and the efficacy of His sacrifice on the cross, as suggested by verse 6. James, on the other hand, could be describing "wandering" of a lesser degree, a failure to be faithful that does not involve a renunciation of faith. It is impossible to be dogmatic about these statements, since the writers do not define their intentions more clearly. But in the case of Hebrews, the warning is clear enough. In the case of James, the hopefulness is equally clear.

Regardless of the exact nature of the "wandering" under consideration, the impossibility of restoring anyone rests not with God but with the person himself. Based on Ezekiel 33.10–11, since God has no pleasure in the death of the wicked, He would clearly welcome back any who would return to Him. The problem is, some become so hardened in their sin and obstinacy that they cannot be persuaded to repent. (Note that Heb 6.4 says it is "impossible to restore" such people, not that it is impossible for them to be forgiven.) If some become so hardened that they can no longer be touched by the thought of Christ's sacrifice for their sins, then there is nothing that can help them; restoration becomes "impossible," a fact which must break the heart of God.

It is important to observe at this point that none of us has the ability to know who has passed that "point of no return" and who has not. That's why James urges us to do all we can to bring back all the wanderers we can from the error of their ways. It isn't our job to determine people's eternal condition in relation to God; it is our job to give them every encouragement to come back to Him.

But How?

Bringing back wanderers from the error of their ways is our responsibility, but how are we to go about it? In Galatians 6.1 Paul offers some general guidelines: "Brothers, if anyone is caught in any transgression, you who are spiritual should restore him in a spirit of gentleness. Keep watch on yourself, lest you too be tempted." The Greek verb translated "restore" is used in Mark 1.19 and Matthew 4.21 for the mending of fishing nets. In 1 Corinthians 1.10 it expresses Christian unity, and in 2 Corinthians 13.11 it is part of an appeal to the Corinthians to "mend your ways." The idea is clear enough: When we "bring back" a wanderer from the error of his ways, we "restore" him to fellowship with God as well as to fellowship with other believers who have maintained the faith. The goal is to get these people back to where they were before they "wandered." Paul says to go about this delicate task "in a spirit of gentleness," not arrogantly as those who could never make the same mistake. People wander from God for all sorts of reasons, and it's up to us to gently try to find out why they left and coax them back, if at all possible. As we do so, Paul says, we must "keep watch on [ourselves], lest we too be tempted." In other words, we must go about this task conscious of our own weaknesses and failures, because only in this frame of mind can we have the humility and grace necessary to lead others back to Christ. Likewise, we should always be on guard so that we do not allow the wanderer to influence us rather than us influencing him!

James offers another important suggestion in this regard: prayer. Verse 16 teaches the importance of mutual confession of sins and promises that prayer's power is effective. So as we seek to restore others, we should, above all, do so prayerfully. This is not to suggest that our prayers will cause someone to be forgiven; James doesn't say we can "pray them into heaven" regardless of whether or not they come back to the Lord. (See 1 John 5.16–17 on this.) Still, we can pray for opportunities to approach them about their sins, and for God to work in their lives in ways that will encourage repentance. We may not always be sure just how praying for sinners "works," but we should still do it.

Just Like Jesus

The final two verses of James also remind us that bringing wanderers back to God is one of the most Christ-like things a person can do, because seeking wanderers and bringing them back was exactly what He was all about. After all, didn't He describe Himself as having come to "seek and to save the lost" (Luke 19.10)? This statement comes at the end of Luke's report of Jesus' encounter with the tax collector, Zacchaeus, a man who was obviously looking for a place with God but who didn't know until Jesus came by that he was also being looked for. And don't forget Jesus' parable about the lost sheep and the shepherd who left ninety-nine sheep safely in the fold to go and look for the lost one (Matt 18.10–14). Just after telling that parable, Jesus said, "If your brother sins against you, go and tell him his fault, between you and him alone. If he listens to you, you have gained your brother" (Matt 18.15). Clearly Jesus was all about reclaiming lost sinners, and that's what He wants His people to be busy doing as well.

Look at what James says we do for a wanderer when we bring him back. First, we "save his soul from death." "Death" here means eternity without God, the worst form of death. Second, we "cover a multitude of sins" by bringing him back. Whose sins? Some suggest that when a believer brings back a wanderer, the reclaimer's own sins are forgiven in return. Those who take this position point to texts such as Proverbs 10.12 ("Hatred stirs up strife, but love covers all offenses"); Ezekiel 3.21 ("But if you warn the righteous person not to sin, and he does not sin he shall surely live, because he took warning, and you will have delivered your soul"); and 1 Timothy 4.16 ("Keep a close watch on yourself and on the teaching. Persist in this, for by so doing you will save both yourself and your hearers"). However, it seems more likely that James refers to the "multitude of sins" of the wanderer, not of the "converter." We seek to reclaim those who have wandered off from God, not for some benefit for ourselves, but because they are in danger of death.

Finally, we should observe that James began this final exhortation with his by-now-familiar formula, "my brothers." The church is a community of believers, a body of people who are responsible for one another's welfare. It is someone "among you" who wanders from God and who needs to be brought back. Dispossessed believers living in a hostile world need to look out for one another in the ways that count the most. Surely this is a significant aspect of the wisdom that James has been encouraging all along.

> *A charge to keep I have, A God to glorify;*
> *A never-dying soul to save, And fit it for the sky.*
> *To serve the present age, My calling to fulfill*
> *Oh, may it all my pow'rs engage To do my Master's will!*
> *Help me to watch and pray, And on Thyself rely.*
> *Assured if I my trust betray, I shall forever die.*

Lowell Mason, "A Charge to Keep I Have"

Also by Tommy South

Just Jesus
The Evidence of History

Few people are able to ignore Jesus. He has devotees and detractors, but hardly anyone is neutral about him. But how much do we know about him? Whether we love him or loathe him, it only makes sense that we know what and whom we're talking about. Just Jesus is about what we can know about Jesus. Jesus isn't just a religious idea but a phenomenon of history. That means we can and should ask about him all of the historical

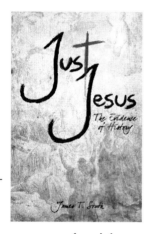

questions we can think of and see which ones can and can't be answered. Fortunately, we're able to learn a lot more about Jesus than most people think. 152 pages, $9.99 (PB).

DE WARD
PUBLISHING COMPANY

For a full listing of DeWard Publishing

Company books, visit our website:

www.deward.com

CPSIA information can be obtained at www.ICGtesting.com
Printed in the USA
BVOW01s2318030614

355275BV00001B/9/P